Fireplace Accessories
Historic and Contemporary

Dona Z. Meilach

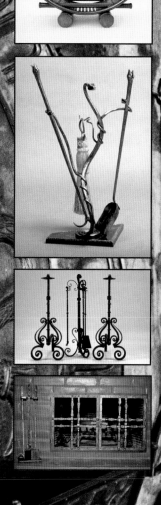

Schiffer Publishing Ltd®

4880 Lower Valley Road, Atglen, PA 19310 USA

Other Art-Craft Books by Dona Z. Meilach
Metalwork and Blacksmithing:
Architectural Ironwork
The Contemporary Blacksmith
Decorative & Sculptural Ironwork
Direct Metal Sculpture
Sculpture Casting *with Dennis Kowal*
Also:
Contemporary Stone Sculpture
Creating Small Wood Objects as Functional Sculpture
How to Create Your Own Designs *with Jay & Bill Hines*
Collage and Assemblage *with Elvie TenHoor*
Macramé- Creative Design in Knotting
Contemporary Art with Wood
Creating Modern Furniture
Woodwork: the New Wave
Batik and Tie Die
Creative Carving
Ethnic Jewelry
Box Art
And others

Front cover, left to right: Tool set, Christopher Thomson. Fire screen, Christopher Thompson. Fire screen, Glenn F. Gilmore. Fire screen, Glenn F. Gilmore. Surround, David Tuthill.
Back cover, clockwise: Tool set, Jerry A, Coe. Fire screen and tool set, Glenn F. Gilmore. Fire screen, Glenn F. Gilmore. Kiva Screen, tool set, log basket, Christopher Thomson.
Title page: Large stove, C. Carl Jennings. Top to bottom: Fire screen, Joe Miller. Log basket, Paul Margetts. Toolset, Joseph Anderson. Tool set, andirons, Stephen Bondi. Fire screen, Stephen Bondi.
Spine: Tool set, Dan Nauman

Copyright © 2002 by Dona Z. Meilach
Library of Congress Catalog Control Number: 2002103256

Designed by Bonnie M. Hensley
Cover design by Bruce M. Waters
Type set in ZapfHumnst BT/Benguiat Bk BT

ISBN: 0-7643-1615-X
Printed in China

Published by Schiffer Publishing Ltd.
4880 Lower Valley Road
Atglen, PA 19310
Phone: (610) 593-1777; Fax: (610) 593-2002
E-mail: Schifferbk@aol.com
Please visit our web site catalog at **www.schifferbooks.com**
We are always looking for people to write books on new and related subjects. If you have an idea for a book, please contact us at the above address.

This book may be purchased from the publisher.
Include $3.95 for shipping. Please try your bookstore first.
You may write for a free catalog.

In Europe, Schiffer books are distributed by
Bushwood Books
6 Marksbury Ave. Kew Gardens
Surrey TW9 4JF England
Phone: 44 (0)20 8392-8585; Fax: 44 (0)20 8392-9876
E-mail: Bushwd@aol.com
Free postage in the UK. Europe: air mail at cost.
Please try your bookstore first.

Dan Nauman

Dedication

To each person who has earned the title of artist black-smith, and especially to the artist blacksmiths whose work appears on these pages.

"Creativity is allowing yourself to make mistakes. Art is knowing which ones to keep."

Scott Adams (1957 -)
United States cartoonist and author of *The Dilbert Principle*

"There is no place more delightful than one's own fireplace"
Marcus Tullius Cicero (106BC - 3BC)
Roman statesman, scholar, and orator

John Phillips

Acknowledgments

I thank the people who sent in a slew of heart-warming (hearth-warming?) responses when they learned I was gathering photos for this book. Each person was so enthusiastic and helpful that, in realty, they all deserve the title "consultant."

I especially thank Stephen Bondi, for always "being there" to answer questions, and provide feedback and encouragement. He graciously made his collection of slides from historical sources in Italy available and contacted present day Italian artist blacksmiths for their excellent examples. He also read and commented on a near final draft of the manuscript.

David W. Koenig joyfully shared photos of the Samuel Yellin andirons he had purchased from an antique dealer. They set us both on sleuthing paths to find out more about them.

I believe I took undue advantage of Dan Nauman's offer to elaborate on any aspect of blacksmithing and fireplace accessories. He patiently "talked" to me via E-mail and offered several valid suggestions based on his extensive experience with clients and commissions.

Lars Stanley tapped into his familiarity with the gallery scene to offer a list of "dos" for artist blacksmiths seeking outlets for their work. The same information applies to people who want to own individualized fire accessories, and how to work with a gallery.

Richard Schrader thoroughly enjoyed going through the more than 1000 photos that came in to help select the pieces that would represent the best examples of work by today's artists. Unfortunately, space limitations and photo quality necessitated culling several excellent examples.

I'm sure my readers will enjoy David E. Wilson's andiron and screen drawings as much I enjoyed assigning them as a leitmotif to each chapter.

I want to thank Jock Dempsey for making my needs known to the hundreds of readers who access his Web site, The Anvils Ring, www.anvilfire.com. That source is probably most responsible for contacting artists in various parts of the world. I was pleased, too, to dig into my archives for photos I had taken through the years, never realizing I would write a book on fireplace objects.

I enjoyed making contact with people at several historic hotels. Thanks to Mary Billingsly, Public Relations Officer of Historic Hotels of America. She led me to Sue Anderson, Jekyll Island Club, Jekyll Island, Georgia; Ginger Gilliam of Lou Hammond & Assoc. representing the Hotel Jerome, Aspen, Colorado; Allison Marshall, the Grove Park Inn, Asheville, North Carolina; and Timothy Fox and Janina Czarnecki of the Bishop's Lodge, Santa Fe, New Mexico. My thanks to all of you for sharing books, photos, and background on your hotels.

My daughter, Susan Seligman, who has been exposed to my art/craft book manuscripts for many years, always does a great job of blue penciling

items, asking questions that make me take a second look at a sentence, a concept, or a fact.

A special thanks to Nancy and Bill Veillette, and David Court, for the chronological photos of the restoration of an Early American stove, and to Stefan Dürst for his photo series of forging and raising tools. Chris Axelsson, John Phillips, Jan Sanchez, Lars Stanley, and David Tuthill also kept a photo log of their fireplace installations for which I am truly grateful. Thanks, too, to Jean-Pierre Masbanji who insisted I take a weekend vacation to visit him and his family, and shoot a few photos at his forge high in the hills above Santa Barbara, California.

I bow in appreciation to the many blacksmiths who have learned to take creditable photos of their work, especially after attending a workshop I presented at the ABANA Conference in 2001. And another bow to all the photographers whose work is represented here.

My appreciation to Nancy and Peter Schiffer for their continuing confidence and encouragement, and to their staff for the care and attention they pay to the production of a book.

My love and gratitude to my husband, Dr. Melvin M. Meilach. He has finally given up asking me to slow down. He continues to dish out patience and is resigned to the fact that meals will be late and that vacations will consist of photo shoots and interviews.

Dona Z. Meilach
Carlsbad, California, 2002

Jeff Fetty

Jerry A. Coe

Preface

It seems uncanny that there would be a topic today that hasn't already filled the pages of a book. Much to my surprise, that was the case with fireplace accessories, items that have been around for several centuries. Fireplaces? Yes. Mantels? Yes. Stonework? Yes. Chimneys? Yes. But the tools one uses to tend the fire? The screens that enclose the fire openings? None. I found only a few examples in a book from England, and drawings of Colonial fireplace accessories in books on early American furnishings.

The idea for this book germinated as a result of many fireplace accessory photos I had received for my earlier book, *The Contemporary Blacksmith*. In that book, I could devote only one chapter to the subject and was dismayed that more of the innovative examples couldn't be shown. When word went out that I was writing this book, a flood of examples arrived along with lengthy letters about the artists' inspirations, techniques, and experiences.

My research revealed that in the year 2000 over 400,000 fireplaces were installed. People were buying mass produced screens and tools from local hardware stores and the few fireplace specialty stores that existed. I was already championing the renaissance of ironwork and here was another direction, another branch of the art form being done by the growing number of talented artist blacksmiths. The public had to be made aware of their options, how, and where to find the people involved.

The result is this book containing over 400 photos of historical and modern fireplace accessories from more than 100 artist blacksmiths in nine countries. It offers ideas, techniques, and inspirational design examples that are sure to excite architects, homeowners, interior decorators, furniture dealers, collectors, gallery owners, museum directors, artist blacksmiths, and those involved in restoration and remodeling work.

I believe that the examples shown will emphasize the premise that functional objects can be sculpture and that the blacksmith is an artist .

Contents

Glenn F. Gilmore

Chapter 1

Fireplaces and Their Accessories

Douglas E. Wilson. Drawing for leaf andirons.

Ever since primitive man rubbed two sticks of wood together and created fire, he has found a need for a place to make and hold a fire. Whether for warmth, light, cooking, or a romantic effect, fireplaces have a long and fascinating history. No matter if the fire was built in a pit dug in the sand, a mud oven, a log cabin, a campfire, a modest home, a mansion, or a palatial living room, it became a gathering place, and an activity center.

In the days before gas, electricity, and central heating, the fireplace was already a focal point and dominant decorative item. Today, homes are built around a fireplace, or a fireplace is added for decoration, nostalgia, ambiance, and because it adds value to a house.

What is the magic of a fireplace? Few people can resist its inviting and mesmerizing effects; the enchantment of flickering flames, crackling fire, and arousing aroma. For some the fire beckons as a place of solitude and privacy; a cozy spot where one can curl up on a soft chair with a favorite novel and a glass of wine. Our pets, too, are lured by the warmth and inclined to doze off in front of the hearth.

With the fireplace, one also needs accessories. Our ancestors needed hooks to hang pots for cooking, and spits to turn food as it cooks. Yesterday's and today's fireplaces need grates to hold burning logs, baskets to hold freshly cut wood, fireplace guards, doors, screens of glass and mesh, and decorative ironwork designs. There are andirons, and fireplace cleaning tools that are as intricately made as fine furniture. Fireplace sets include shovels, pokers, brooms, and stands for them with handles that may have wonderfully carved figures, twists, and elaborate shapes.

Antique fireplace accessories are valuable collector's items. Their designs have followed the same historical art trends as other artwork. Some are ornately baroque and Elizabethan, some have birds, dragon and gargoyle heads. Several date from Art Nouveau, Art Deco, Arts & Crafts, and Prairie styles from about 1900 to the 1930s time period. There are regional examples from France, Spain, Germany, and Colonial America.

Opposite page: Glenn F. Gilmore. Free standing Rose Fire Screen of copper with stainless steel mesh. A matching metal rose blossom was made for the vase on the mantel. The flowers complement the room's floral motif. The screen is 36" wide, 30 " high. *Photo, McNabb Studio*

Fireplace screens, designed to contain embers and keep them from damaging carpeting near a hearth, often have themes worked into them. Historical examples ncluded biblical stories, mythological symbols, or designs from nature. Some carried stylized initials of the home's owners or a family crest. Modern fireplace hardware often exhibits detailing along the same lines as historical examples with the added concepts of free form, geometric, and asymmetrical designs.

Fireplaces can be built into a wall, free standing at the side, or in the center of a room. They may be created as a stove that is as sculptural as a statue. They can be designed with plain facades or heavily embellished with columns, figures, plant shapes, and symbols.

Not surprisingly, options and reasons for a fireplace have changed with the times. A fireplace may be made of clay, stone, brick, tile, plaster, or wood. In many societies, and as far back as Roman times, fuel might have been dung patties, peat, coal, twigs, leaves, or wood, depending on climate and availability. In some countries, those fuels are still the mainstay. Fuel choices in the modern home may be cured hardwood, natural or manufactured gas, electricity, oil, sawdust pellets, coal or peat. Solar stoves are becoming increasingly popular in sunny areas of the world. The heat supplied by the sun's rays is focused by means of a concave reflector.

Cured hardwood burns longer, hotter, and cleaner than most softwood, and produces less creosote buildup (a fire hazard) in the chimney. Some areas of the United States have banned the use of wood burning fireplaces to reduce emissions, and to conserve wood. The alternative for these areas is cleaner burning natural gas. If a fireplace is not available, one can simulate the effect of a fire on a television set by playing a video of a fire burning. There's no heat emitted, but it will increase electric bills. One can cook by it if the TV is in the kitchen.

There's an adage about wood that says, "Wood warms you twice." That means once when you cut it, and again when you burn it. Ready to burn logs are easy to purchase. But to some the process of "making wood" involves all the senses.

Dan Nauman explains: "I have enjoyed the pleasure of taking a team of horses pulling a bob sled through freshly fallen snow to the wood lot to 'make wood.' In the north where I live, the best time for making wood is in the winter when the ground is frozen solid and firm. The intense weight of a full load of wood at any other time of the year would cause the vehicle to get bogged in moist soil. In winter, the horses pull effortlessly through a sea of snow, icicles forming on their whiskers, and steam jetting out their nostrils. We arrive at a wood lot, and make our selections for felling trees. After a few hours of hard work cutting and stacking the freshly chopped wood upon the sled, I stop the saw briefly for a sandwich. I sit upon a stump, explore the treetops, listen to a red squirrel's chatter, and inhale the aromas. The experience of working with the team out in the dead of winter enhances the pleasures of a wood burning fire."

There's the romance and then the reality about making a fire. For some people, making a fire is a necessity, not romance. The camper in the woods needs a small fire for cooking, for light, and warmth. There are women who bake flat bread in brick and mud ovens. Even then, children tend to gather around the ovens in rural areas throughout the world waiting for the hot warm circles of baked bread. In nomadic cultures, bread is often baked in a hole dug into the ground that is lined with an oil can, or a tube of metal or clay, rather than in above the ground ovens.

In many cultures, fire has sacred connotations. Early sun-worshipping peoples revered fire that they deemed an earthly representative of the sun. Ancient Greeks considered fire one of four essential elements from which all things were composed, along with water, earth, and air. When Zeus mistreated man by planning to deprive him of fire, Prometheus smuggled the precious flame from the Gods and gave it to man.

Primitive ovens may be made of brick, mud, or other indigenous materials. The fire is built in the bottom of the hollow using twigs and leaves. Round flat breads are baked on the inside wall of the oven. Photographed in Mardin, Turkey. *Photo, author*

The Greek God, Hephaestus, the son of Zeus and Hera, forged thunderbolts that were hurled in anger from Olympus to tame and rule a world occupied by rebellious peoples. The blacksmith of early Greek mythology had almost uncanny abilities; he was pictured as taming fire to his will. He turned the earth's ores into magic for forging invincible weapons and simple tools.

In Roman culture, Vesta, the goddess of the hearth, was highly regarded in every household from early times to the beginning of Christianity. Vulcan was the Roman god of fire who caught Venus and her lover, Ares, in a net of iron. He fashioned weapons for war and gold platters for serving foods. The discovery and the uses of fire helped develop the arts of metalwork and ceramics, and fostered huge advances in civilization.

During European wars, the blacksmith was essential in the army's entourage. He was indispensable for shoeing horses, making stirrups and other equestrian gear, fashioning and repairing guns and knives, and making cooking vessels.

Nomadic societies may bake their flat breads in a hole dug in the earth and lined with an oilcan or metal tube. Photographed near Van, Turkey. *Photo, author*

From the Renaissance period and forever after, blacksmiths also turned their hands to decorative items such as staircases, gates, and fences. Fireplace hardware followed and, by the 17th Century, ornate fire screens appeared, but their design has not been emphasized nor their makers extolled. Rather the fireplace and the mantel with intricately carved *putti*, columns, heraldic symbols, and gilded moldings, garnered the main attention from architects and designers.

The Colonial American blacksmith was more involved in making farming equipment (turning weapons into plowshares). Sample work entries from records of 18th and 19th Century blacksmiths included altering harrow teeth, plating a plough, mending a bridle bar and hook, repairing an axe, making hinges, welding a chain, and shoeing horses. The blacksmith undoubtedly made objects for the hearth but these were rarely noted. Museum holdings indicate that such items were primarily functional, though many were simply and beautifully decorated by the blacksmith. The most frequent needed fireplace items were a pair of andirons. Or perhaps, because of their sturdiness, they have lasted through the centuries.

A *stufa*, or stove, is a piece of functional furniture used in central European homes. It is often made of blue and white intricately designed Majolica tiles. Photographed in Zurich, Switzerland. *Photo, author*

Bishop's Lodge Resort. The outdoor kiva fireplace made of adobe is from New Mexico, but similar fireplaces and materials are used in Spanish country homes and in hot countries such as Greece and Morocco. *Courtesy, Bishop's Lodge Resort, New Mexico*

Colonial Dinner, Lahaska, Pennsylvania. The colonial fireplace is still popular in eastern and southern states that were first settled in America. Restaurant and hotel decorators try to find original accessories, or replicate historical items. *Courtesy, Colonial Dinner, Peddler's Village, Lahaska, Pennsylvania*

Hotel Jerome. Aspen, Colorado. Fireplaces in early western United States hotels were eclectic. Furnishings had little resemblance to the colonial architecture of the East Coast. This room from the Hotel Jerome in Aspen, Colorado, opened in 1889. Much of it was restored in the 1960s. *Courtesy, Hotel Jerome, Aspen, Colorado*

Samuel Yellen. One of the pair of Yellin's andirons with his name inscribed. Often a chevron design was stamped on his andirons indicating they were made in his shop, probably sometime between 1920 and 1940. Spit hooks are attached to the uprights. Collection, David W. Koenig. *Photo, Jason Neumann*

Each andiron consisted of three parts; a horizontal bar, legs to raise it above the ground, and a tall front bar, or shaft. The horizontal bars held logs to be burned, and the tall front bars prevented the logs from rolling off. The front bars varied in height according to the size of the fireplace opening. Tall andirons used in kitchen fireplaces often had hooks attached on the front or back of the shaft to support a roasting spit. The hooks were called spit hooks. Many large andirons also had basket shaped tops used for warming bottles of spirits, and keeping food warm. For small fireplaces used in bedrooms, the andirons were topped with round or faceted finials that were either straight up or tilted forward.

Kitchen fireplaces also had hardware called a crane, or a sway, that could be swung over the fire for cooking and then forward so that pots could be removed or emptied. A horizontal bar with a support brace was attached that held pothooks, called trammels, from which various pots and kettles could be hung over the fire. The smithy, too, often made the pots until the time cast iron pots were mass-produced in factories. No need to have them fancy.

Angelo Bartolucci. Reproduction of an old andiron shows the spit hooks used to hold the horizontal bars on which animals or meats were roasted, or cooking pots were hung. *Photo, artist*

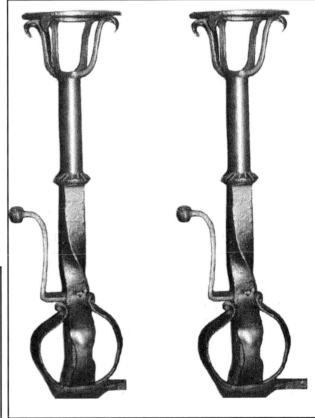

Jekyll Island Club Hotel. Andirons from the Jekyll Island Club Hotel, from the early 1920s, are not signed, but may have been fashioned by the Yellin shop. Yellin's business had flourished along the eastern seaboard at the time the Jekyll Hotel was built. *Courtesy Jekyll Island Club Hotel, Jekyll Island, Georgia*

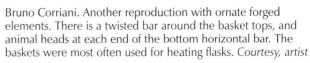

Bruno Corriani. Another reproduction with ornate forged elements. There is a twisted bar around the basket tops, and animal heads at each end of the bottom horizontal bar. The baskets were most often used for heating flasks. *Courtesy, artist*

13

Dan Nauman. Fireplace cranes were important accessories for the blacksmith to make. They held cooking vessels that could be raised or lowered, and swung in and out of the fireplace. Today artist blacksmiths make them for reconstructing historical sites and reproducing the old in a new building. This is a version of a crane from the 17th -18th Century for a restoration. *Photo, artist*

Keith A. Leavitt. Whale Tale andiron. Andirons built for the restoration of a 1790s house. Using "artistic license" a few variations were made; the "spit racks" hold a reversible warming tray and the traditional round ball tops are whale tail finials. *Photo, Steven Dunn.*

14

Decorative fire doors, screens, and tools are a relatively modern development. Occasionally a set of fire tools shows up in antique shops and these may have carved animal heads. It is hard to authenticate when and where they originated. Art history books occasionally show one or two fire screens from well-known metalworkers and architects such as Edgar Brandt of France, Carlo Rizzarda of Italy, and Samuel Yellin in America. Even Frank Lloyd Wright is known to have designed fireplace accessories to accompany his interior designs. These only begin to show up in books after the 1920s. It's more revealing to observe that screens and tools were not pictured or noted. Certainly, they were rarely listed in an index, as such, in books dealing with the history of a particular art period, or even with a specific architect or artist.

Many early fireplaces were fitted with a fireback and they are still in use in European homes. A fireback is a panel that protects the hearth's chimney wall from the fire and throws some heat back into the room. Several beautifully designed cast iron firebacks are displayed in European and American museums that date from about the mid 1500s. These were created in foundries using a sand casting method. Patterns were stamped into a mass of wet sand on the foundry floor. Molten iron was poured into the resulting depressions and allowed to cool. The Victoria & Albert Museum, London, England, has an "Armada" fireback from 1588 with a scene that is believed to represent the defeat of the Spanish Armada at that time.

Carlo Rizzarda. The center portion of a symmetrical fireplace screen by this early 20th Century Italian ironworker illustrates precise scrollwork and carved birds. Copper detailing adds color to the otherwise black iron. *Photo, Stephen Bondi*

Firebacks used today may not all be cast iron. Ermanno and Alessandro Ervas, of Italy, produce beautiful firebacks for new fireplaces and for restoration work. They use hot forging methods, and then work the designs by chiseling and chasing in the cold metal. Those shown have an Egyptian influence.

Modern artisans sometimes create decorative panels to use as "summer screens." John Rais' version of the summer screen is a sheet of decorative forged bronze that is inserted in the fire door during the seasons when a fire will not be built.

Ermanno and Alessandro Ervas. Forged and chiseled fire back with facing couple based on an Egyptian painting. *Courtesy, artist*

Carlo Rizzarda. Fireplace fenders, or guards, were popular for traditional large fireplaces, rather than doors or screens. They were used when the area in front of the fireplace was large. The idea was to prevent embers from reaching the carpeting. They may still be used when people replicate furnishings of an early period. *Photo, Stephen Bondi*

Ermanno and Alessandro Ervas. Forged fire backs with a bird. Erva's designs are worked in the cold metal using chiseling and chasing techniques. *Courtesy, artist*

Peter Paul Rubens House. The house of the artist, Peter Paul Ruben's, in Antwerp, dates from 1610. Most likely, this cast iron screen and andirons were installed in the grand fireplace during a restoration between 1939 and 1946. *Photo, Shelley Lipman*

A nebulous history of modern screens and hardware in America dates back to about the 1920s when blacksmiths who immigrated to the United States from Europe began to produce decorative and functional items for the burgeoning building industries. Samuel Yellin on the East Coast, and Edward Trinkkeller on the West Coast, created decorative fireplace pieces that can be identified by a brand mark or because records exist. Yellin's designs, often signed and dated, were for wealthy clients who built hotels and mansions in New York, Georgia, and along the Eastern seaboard. Trinkkeller's pieces show up at the Hearst Castle, in California, from about 1928.

Edgar Brandt, a French artist blacksmith, exhibited his work in the United States in 1924 at the same time Yellin's shop was booming. Interestingly, Brandt's work was launched in America by a company that translated his wonderfully sinuous Art Deco ironwork into designs on silk.

Edward Gustave Trinkkeller. Fireplace screen 1926-28, produced for the Hearst Castle, San Simeon, California. Early fireplace screens often had mythological images that related a story. This one depicts Satan dancing around a fire. Note that the andirons have basket shaped tops. A cooking pot is suspended from the poker that rests across two spit hooks. *Courtesy, Hearst Castle/ Hearst San Simeon State Historical Monument. Photo, Victoria Caragliano*

Cast iron andirons were usually imported from England for the grand hotels in the United States. These are from the Castle Greene, built in 1896, in Pasadena, California. *Photo, author*

Samuel Yellen. Andirons from about 1920. Samuel Yellin is probably among the first ironworkers in the United States who has name recognition among artists and metalworkers. Note the similarity of these andirons to those in the Trinkkeller screen. Collection, David W. Koenig. *Photo, Jason Neumann*

Chimneys

When we think of fireplace accessories, we may overlook the importance of the chimney; but once fires were brought inside, the chimney became an important structural element in a house. While chimneys are not the focus of this book, it's interesting to take a quick glimpse into their development.

Chimneys were not built with any style in England before 1529 due to a Papal chimney tax levied on their construction. After the Reformation, intricately patterned brick chimneys and ornate fireplaces evolved. The fireplace surround was often made of plaster instead of marble. Plaster was cheaper and molds were made from which multiple units could be reproduced.

The most unusual, and well-known, chimneys appeared in the Tudor period; they are the twisted brick chimneys for Cardinal Wolsey's Hampton House in England. These wonderfully whimsical looking single and double chimneystacks carry the fire residue from scores of fireplaces throughout the huge building.

Antonio Gaudí's, Casa Milá in Barcelona, Spain, built in 1905 to 1907, is a crowning achievement in chimneys that has not yet been equaled or surpassed. They are fancifully shaped, all different, some in brick, some covered in tile. Walking on the building's rooftop is like traversing through a fairyland.

Along Portugal's Algarve area on the southern coast, decorative chimney pots are often in the shape of small architectural structures. Sometimes, ironwork decorations appear on chimney tops in Italy. To the untrained eye, they look like weather vanes but they have no directional notations for north, south, east, or west. They are purely decorative.

Today's chimneys, mostly rectangular in shape, may be designed in intricate stone and brick patterns. One can drive through any modern housing development and see the variety possible. Stonemasons, not iron-workers, create these fine architectural enhancements.

Perhaps the most whimsical, best known, and recognized chimneys are those of the Spanish architect, Antonio Gaudí, who transformed the landscape and skyline of Barcelona, Spain, with his Casa Milá. The chimneys are made of cement and some have colorful tile coverings. *Photo, author*

Antonio Gaudí. Gaudí's chimneys were particularly unique at the time they were built. Until then traditional Romanesque and Elizabethan styles dominated throughout Europe. *Photo, author*

Chimneys in the Algarve, along the southern coast of Portugal, have a Moorish influence that can be seen in their cylindrical or prismatic shapes, and in the geometric designs penetrating the clay. The chimneys are white washed, and may have details painted to accentuate their ornamentation. Some Italian buildings have similar chimney pots but they differ in that they are designed to resemble miniature houses. *Photo, author*

Tudor style brick twisted chimneys of Cardinal Thomas Wolsey's Royal Palace, Hampton Court, about 1550, outside of London, England. *Photo, author*

Ermanno and Alessandro Ervas. Often the blacksmith is called upon to make decorative designs for chimney tops in Italy. This is not a weather vane as there are no directional symbols for N.S.E.W. *Photo, artist*

Ilya Magid. The stonemason today may make intricately designed chimneys inspired by historical versions such as this twisted Tudor style chimney. *Photo, artist*

Ilya Magid. Double chimney with patterned stonework. *Photo, artist*

Ilya Magid. Herringbone pattern chimney. *Photo, artist*

Emil Benes and Associates, Architects. A contemporary California house in the French Provincial style includes decorative chimney pots as an architectural element. *Photo, author*

Buying Fireplace Accessories

Fireplace doors, screens, and tools are readily available at specialized fireplace shops, furniture stores, and where fine hardware accessories are sold. Mass produced hardware is very affordable and will enhance a fireplace by virtue of its being there. The items may be made of iron with bronze, brass, or copper accents and will do the job for which they are purchased.

The customized accessory, made by an artist craftsman, is harder to come by because you have to find the people who make them. More likely, you will find them by word of mouth, by checking the yellow pages of your phone book under metal workers or blacksmiths, or by contacting the associations listed in the Appendix, Resources. After making the contact, you may want to interview a few crafts people to see their earlier work and determine whether he or she can create something in the style you want. It's also important for the crafts person to see the site so that a custom unit can be designed.

Country Inns & Suites. A gas burning fireplace in a modern hotel represents a "Country Style" that is difficult to define. It combines a hint of Colonialism and old world charm. Mainly, like all fireplaces, it is cozy and welcoming whether one has just returned from skiing, or must catch up with work on a laptop computer at the end of a day. *Courtesy, Country Inns & Suites.*

Chapter 2

Inspiration and Perspiration

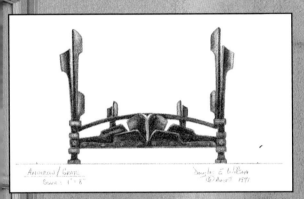

Douglas E. Wilson. Drawing for andirons with bitterns.
Courtesy, artist

Designs for fireplace accessories are so varied, one must ask, where do artists and designers get their ideas? Many are based on historical perspectives and work in other media. Designs from nature such as, trees, mountains, animals, insects, and fish, are popular and often reflect a client's interests. Some are strictly geometric. Often an idea springs from the artist's imagination. In all cases, the ideas must conform to the materials, tools, and techniques available and, ultimately, the artist's ability to control and manipulate them. Mix these all together and, like the alphabet that creates thousands of words in one language and many more in other languages, the results can be infinite. Once an artist envisions a project's approach, he usually sketches it out, then shows it to the client until both agree on a design.

This chapter provides an overview of how ideas evolve, how they are transformed from the artist's head, through his hands, into existence. You will appreciate the work involved in making this existence happen. Your appreciation of fireplace hardware will multiply to the point where you may never again see a fireplace, its doors, and its hardware, without being aware of its existence and how it came to be. You'll observe fireplaces in shelter magazine photos and in publications devoted to architecture and interior design. These publications, in turn, can provide design ideas for people who want to create distinctive fireplaces.

Christopher Thomson. Custom kiva fireplace screen, tool set, and log holder. The movable screen has a handle at the top, rivets, and supports as ornamentation and function. The tool bracket is purposely left rough. The end of each tool is wound around the handle portion for function and decoration. *Photo, Peter Vitale*

Some artists work in traditional designs, taking their cue and inspiration from historical periods such as Renaissance, French Provincial, Classicism, Post Classicism, Baroque, Tudor, Victorian, Colonial, Art Nouveau, Art Deco, Craftsman, Modern, Post Modern, and so forth. The artist selects styles that will complement the environment in which the accessories will be used whether it's an apartment, private home, estate, castle, hotel, or boardroom.

A client may have a favorite decorative item that he wants replicated in the fire doors and hardware. It might be a detail in a Persian rug that can be repeated in a hinge motif. It could be an African sculpture with detailing captured in a fireplace frame. A hobby or a special interest could become the subject, such as baseball, golf, and fishing, the reflection of a nearby mountain, or the geography and history of a region. It's obvious that Christopher Thomson's adobe fireplace reflects a southwestern theme. Thomson's custom designed accessories for a kiva fireplace screen, tools, and log holder are gutsy, yet simple. Their only ornamentation is the rivet heads that are functional and decorative, and the bent loops at the top of the log basket.

A stained glass window with tracery and anthemion leaves is the type of traditional design often used as inspiration for ironwork. The same elements used here appear in the fireplace screen by Jean-Pierre Masbanji for a traditionally styled home. Window detail from the Museum of Decorative Arts, Prague, Czech Republic, built in 1885, in the Neo-Renaissance style. *Photo, author*

Jean-Pierre Masbanji, an artist blacksmith who studied in France, easily interprets his French Classical background for people who decorate in French motifs. His beautifully flowing forms in iron are masterfully crafted. When discussing the design for the screen shown, the client asked him, "What do you see?" Masbanji responded, "I see a dark trimmed mirror frame defined with leaves, a bronze patina with variegated hues of gray and pewter shades in the mantel."

Masbanji's French style bi-folding doors have a fixed top arch designed to enhance the room's décor. The hand-forged iron has stainless steel screening sandwiched between the frame and a backing frame. Anthemion leaves are hand raised bronze using repoussé techniques and finished in Statuary Antique Bronze coloring with bronze highlights. Waxed charcoal gray pewter tones are on the iron frame and details.

The entire screen took about six weeks to complete. Each anthemion leaf required four to eight hours to develop from flat metal to shaped and veined leaf, then finishing. This will give you some idea of the time and effort involved. It's difficult to convey in the pages of a book the equipment used, the experience in working metal, the physical work, and the perspiration expended to complete such a project.

Jean-Pierre Masbanji. The frame is made first.

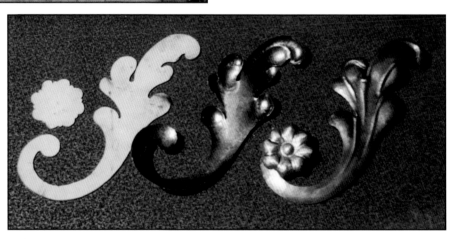

Jean-Pierre Masbanji. Patterns, cut steel blanks, and finished anthemia are made using the repoussé process. Each anthemion may take half to a full day to make. Leaves are cut from 1.2-mm bronze sheet, then shaped, and planished. Veins are raised freehand over a stake using repoussé.

Jean-Pierre Masbanji. Bi-folding fireplace doors in the French Neo-Classic style with tracery and anthemion leaves. Hinges and handles are hand forged. Bronze finish. *Photo, James Chen*

Jean-Pierre Masbanji. 1. Preliminary sketches for the French Neo-Classic doors. His were made to get a feel of the overall positive and negative spaces in relation to scale.

Jean-Pierre Masbanji. 2 .The second sketches were to show his idea to the client.

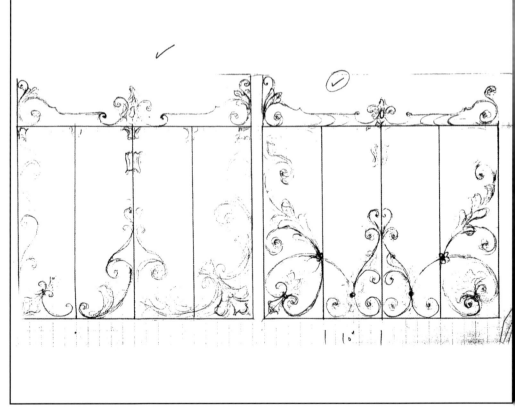

Jean-Pierre Masbanji. 4. A full-scale final drawing is made, and then placed on cardboard. As the parts are formed, they are laid out on the cardboard drawing to be assembled.

Jean-Pierre Masbanji. 3. A more detailed drawing was prepared for presentation and site verification. Even then, changes may occur. The client wanted the top altered from the drawing.

John Phillips and Chris Axelsson have attempted to show several steps and the work involved in creating a fire screen. In Chapter 4, Stefan Dürst illustrates how a shovel is raised. The artist blacksmith generally works in a shop with a forge that is fired with coal or gas. A bar of metal is heated in the forge to high temperatures, about 2500 Fahrenheit, until it is in a malleable state. While the heat remains in the metal, the blacksmith puts it on his anvil and begins to hammer it into a shape, handling it with tongs and other tools. When it cools, the process is repeated. It is hot work, hard work, sweaty work that accounts for the perspiration along with the inspiration.

After the metal is shaped it must be fabricated. Parts are joined by welding, riveting, screwing, or other means, so the craftsman must have a wealth of techniques at his fingertips. What he doesn't know he must figure out. Everything must follow a plan and be accurate. The artist blacksmith must be a Renaissance man, able to design, sell, negotiate, engineer, create, install, and collect his money. Not an easy set of talents, yet many do it very successfully.

John Phillips. In the following series, John Phillips illustrates that forging is only one of many disciplines the artist must use. He must be an engineer and a welder, too.

The" before" picture in this remodeled home. The old fireplace is ready for a facelift with a set of decorative doors. *Photo series, Mark Vaughn*

John Phillips. After measuring the space into which the doors must fit, Phillips makes a cardboard template. The metal frame parts are laid out to match the template, and then placed, and clamped together.

John Phillips. Steel for the fascia and bracing are heated in the forge to prepare them for shaping and texturing.

John Phillips. The heated steel is textured with a power hammer. Different textures for the parts are achieved by changing the tool above the anvil. Hinges and handles are made and installed on the appropriate pieces.

John Phillips. The frame parts are welded.

John Phillips. After all parts are assembled, cleaned, and polished, the finished doors are mounted in the space and, finally, the screen is completed. The two side sections are stationery, the center door is hinged. *Photo series, Mark Vaughn*

The C-scroll shape is a basic form appearing in ironwork. It's easy to see how it is used in Masbanji's French style fire screen. It is evident in the screens by C. Carl Jennings and Stephen Bondi as well as the original Art Nouveau screen shown, each incorporating it with variations. Some scrolls are wide-open C's, some have short ends, others have longer ends pulled into delicate tendrils, or they may become almost circular with forms and coils within the C shape. Jennings combines his C-scrolls with quatrefoils, Bondi's C-scrolls are wide open and the ends are splayed in a fishtail form. The Art Deco example has the circular shape tightly curled and some are squished into ovals. The basic shape is still the C.

Stephen Bondi. A curved set of fire doors imposes different structural problems and solutions than a flat construction. Traditional C-scrolls are used with stylized wheat sheaves. Bronze detailing is added on the tops of the curves, frame, and handles of the matching tool set. *Photo, artist(©)Bondi Metals*

Other detailing you'll see in examples throughout the book are the fundamental expressive elements of the ironworker. Spiral twists, twists that resemble a pineapple skin, one that has a wheat sheaf design, S-scrolls, fishtail scrolls, coils, pointed ends, ends that are "upset" or hit back on themselves and shaped into pyramids, balls, animal heads, and much more. The artist may use repoussé techniques. Instead of heat forging heavy steel, cold metals such as brass, aluminum, or sheet steel, are shaped over stakes.

C. Carl Jennings. Quatrefoils and C-scrolls are delicately and elegantly constructed. Such traditional shapes can be combined infinitely for fire screens designs. *Photo, Stone and Steccati*

Glenn F. Gilmore. A freestanding fireplace screen with a
diamond motif echoes the design in the surrounding
mantel. C- and S-shaped scrolls are at the top and
bottom, and two of the upright bars have twists. The
three legged hearth tool stand holds the matching tools
with basket handles. *Photo, McNabb Studio*

Variations of the C-scroll appear in this original Art Deco
screen, dating from about 1929. Such designs are often
inspiration for today's fire screens and for many other
items. *Photo, author*

Masbanji's Spanish colonial doors have a permutation of the quatrefoil in the central part of the screen. The theme is repeated on the bottom panel in a closed repoussé shape.

Jerry A. Coe's forged bronze Art Nouveau fire screen illustrates how today's artists take their design cues from past art historical periods. Art Nouveau blossomed at the turn of the 20th Century, mainly in Belgium, then spread throughout Europe under a variety of names until the beginning of World War I. It was characterized by curving lines and shapes taken from flower forms. Coe uses these lines and shapes brilliantly.

Jean-Pierre Masbanji. The accomplished artist blacksmith easily works in several design categories. These doors are for a California home with a Spanish Colonial décor. All surfaces are hand textured, all details hand forged. Indestructible screening is sandwiched and riveted to the frame. A graphite-waxed patina is the finish. *Photo, Wm. B. Dewey*

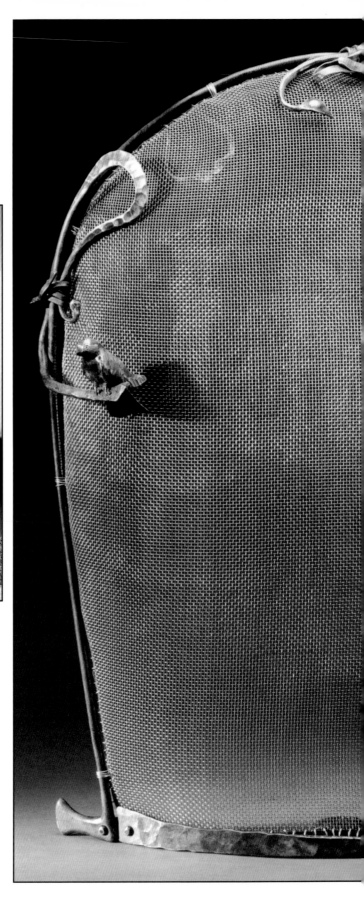

Jerry A. Coe. Forged bronze Art Nouveau screen with a hand carved bird. Extensive hammered textures give the screen its feeling of movement along with the sinuous curved elements, and the shape of the frame. *Photo, Richard Sargent*

Eric Clausen and Michael Bondi also use references to Art Nouveau forms in their incredibly unique approaches to customized fire doors.

Michael Bondi. A maquette, or model, of a set of doors may be fabricated before producing it as a finished work. This maquette, in the Art Nouveau style, was forged and fabricated using bronze, copper, and Monel to achieve different colors and textures. The finished doors will have screening. *Courtesy, artist*

Eric Clausen. The beauty of Art Nouveau influences is that they never seem to go out of style and they retain their freshness and originality. The curving linear elements in different weights extend beyond the frame and become asymmetrical supports. *Photo, artist*

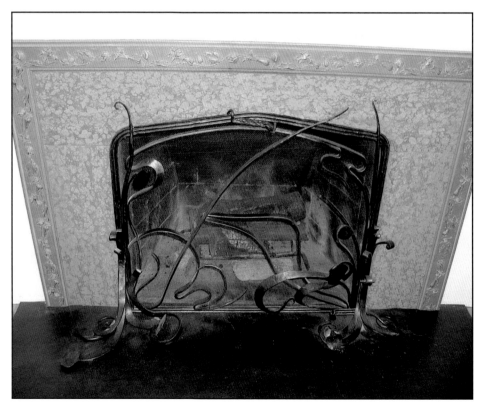

Bob Bergman. Four panel bi-folding door based on a Frank Lloyd Wright prairie style design. To open, the doors fold in half and then to the sides to reveal a folding mesh screen and the fire. A damper at the bottom can control the draft when the doors are closed, making it like a stove. A heat exchange unit is built into the masonry. The catch is magnetic. *Photo, artist*

Chris Axelsson. Detail of a fire screen with oceanic kelp illustrating his approach to making a fire screen. Regardless of the design, the screen must be attached to the frame. Some artists emphasize these attachments as a design motif; others may try to integrate them so they are not obvious. *Courtesy, artist*

Bob Bergman's fireplace doors were designed for a home based on the architecture of Frank Lloyd Wright. The influence was carried through to the accessories. Says Bergman, "This was a typical prairie style house and the design for the fire doors emulated a carpet pattern from a Frank Lloyd Wright house."

John Phillips' photo series of steps involved in creating a pair of fire doors aptly demonstrates the idea of inspiration plus perspiration. In his examples, he shows the iron being heated in a forge then shaping it under the force of a power hammer and installing it.

With so many procedures involved in creating a fireplace enclosure, the process of planning and attaching the screen to the opening is an art in itself. Adding the decorative elements requires another series of procedures after each element is hand forged. Chris Axelsson shared several procedures to help understand the amount of handwork required and to appreciate why custom-made accessories are costly.

Chris Axelsson. Fire screen with oceanic kelp. Axelsson's inspiration is nature itself, but even with the subject changed, a design can combine elements from different art periods such as Classic, Neo-Classic, Empire, Modern, and others. *Courtesy, artist*

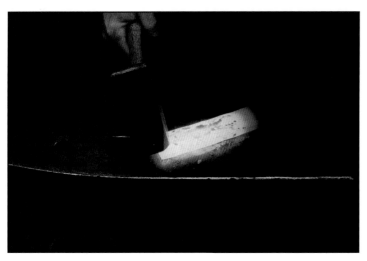

Chris Axelsson 1. The flat bar frame is heated.
Photo series, Valerie Ostenak

4. The most common traditional wire screen cloth is plain steel, usually 6-mesh .035-diameter wire. It is also available in a 7 and 8 size mesh.

2. The edge of the frame is forged into scallops.

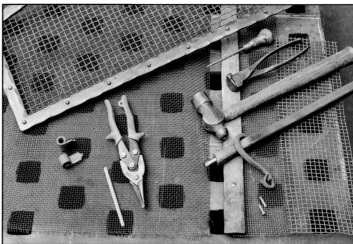

5. Specific tools are needed to assemble the screen to the frame.

3. Holes are drilled for the placement of the rivets.

6. Any imperfections in the wire cloth must be smoothed and flattened.

7. The mesh screen is sandwiched between the frame and a back up piece of flat bar drilled with the same hole spacing for 3/16" diameter rivets.

10. The scroll will be attached to the screen with wires.

8. As the frame is constructed, the rivets protrude about 3/8" of an inch. They will be hammered down and forged to a dome shape.

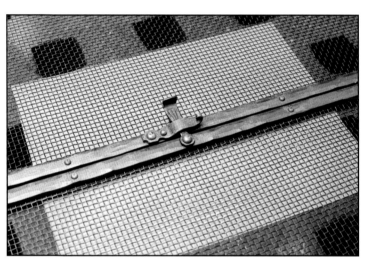

11. A simple latch for a pair of doors. *Photo series, Valerie Ostenak*

9. A forged scroll element; several will be made and attached to the screen.

Chris Axelsson. Fire doors with hinged side fenders illustrate the final construction of a screen, frame, riveting, and decorative additions. After construction is completed, the piece has to be cleaned, and then finished with a patina and wax. *Courtesy, artist*

For anyone planning to commission custom accessories, it is important to know the building codes for your state. In some states, glass doors are mandatory, and there may be other safety codes involved. Be sure the people with whom you work know these codes, and follow them so that there will be no surprises come inspection day.

While European artists were immersing themselves in the Art Nouveau period, American artists often took their cues from influences indigenous to the United States. Steve Lopes made a fireplace for an American Craftsman style bungalow. The Craftsman style, often called the bungalow style, was the dominant residential building form in America in the 1910s and 1920s. Craftsman style houses were notable for their clean and carefully articulated surfaces and Lopes has captured this simplicity in his iron with bronze studded Craftsman style fire doors.

Steve Lopes. Craftsman style fireplace made with bi-folding doors. The frame is iron with hand-forged hinges and handles. Handles and rivets are bronze. *Photo, artist*

Christopher Thomson. Often the artist blacksmith will carry the inspiration for his work into furniture as well as fire screens. Thompson designs coordinated fireplace accessories, bed, blanket bench, mirror frame, and candleholder, all perfectly complementing one another. *Photo, Dave Marlow*

Corrina R. Mensoff. Bamboo fire screen designed for a modern home with Eastern furnishings and architectural details. Iron and copper. Collection, Jill Buckner. *Photo, Jill Buckner*

Corrina R. Mensoff. Bamboo fire screen detail. The artist had to study the nature of the plant, its culms, internodes, and nodes, and then create them in iron by shaping and texturing while retaining the concept of natural growth. *Photo, Jill Buckner*

Chapter 3

Fire Screens and Doors

Plants and Other Organic Designs

Nature's forms are favorite subjects for artists and designers, whether they create a painting, design fabric, shape a clay pot, or carve a block of marble. The artist working in metals taps the same inspiration banks. Plants, animals, fish, and people become popular themes for fireplace screens. Within these themes, the artist may make realistic, stylized, or abstract forms. The basic material most often is mild steel, but bronze, copper, aluminum, and other metals may be used mostly for decoration.

You almost feel you're in a Florida swamp when you study Kirk Sullens large 6' X 6' fireplace doors of steel and copper. Plants overhang Sullens wonderfully detailed copper alligator lolling on a branch. The turtle by Bobby Hood seems unperturbed by the possibility that a flip of the gaiter's tail will send it flying. Randy Wyrick's dragonfly with its green body is at the top of the frame. The screen tells a story, encloses the firebox, and represents a pure sculptural form.

Bamboo is the theme for Corrina R. Mensoff's carefully composed screen for a home with an Oriental motif. The screen doesn't just fill the opening, it extends around, and out from it like a living organic form. Many textures are worked into the bamboo, its leaves, and frame. Before a project is started, it must be meticulously planned, agreed upon by artist and client, and measurements and drawings made before a piece of metal is cut.

Douglas E. Wilson.
Sketch for fire screen with birds. *Courtesy, artist*

Kirk Sullens with Robert E. M. Hood and Randy Wyrick. Forged and fabricated fireplace doors of steel and copper by Kirk Sullens. Sullens' alligator is copper. The turtle was forged and fabricated by Robert E. M. Hood, and the dragonfly by Randy Wyrick. The doors are 6' wide, 6' high. *Photo, Chris Gray*

In her Fern and Hosta freestanding screen, Mensoff's design evolved from photographs taken in the client's garden, and by discussing the client's personal aesthetic. Mensoff's work in copper lends itself to the abstraction of nature so when she presented three sketches using abstract shapes of their plants, the clients were delighted. The hosta plant has heart shaped shiny, distinctly veined leaves that Mensoff created in copper using forging and repoussé techniques. Placing the plants on either side formed a frame for the fire. The screen is an additional work of art in a home that displays an impressive art collection.

John Rais' freestanding fire screens have interchangeable fronts. This unit has screening but it also has a bronze plate that can be inserted during seasons when the fire is not lit. Rais shapes the stylized sprigs then lays them out, and marks them for positioning before welding.

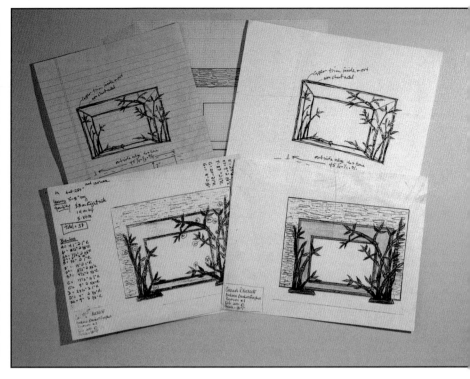

Corrina R. Mensoff. Drawings for the bamboo fire screen. The design evolved through a series of drawings that conceptualized the form. For the final presentation, full-scale drawings were rendered. *Courtesy, artist*

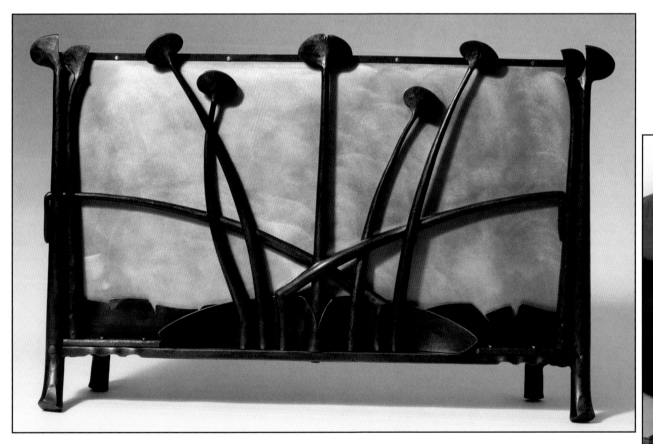

John Rais. Stylized fireplace screen /sculpture shows an interchangeable bronze plate that is inserted in a season when the fire is not lit. *Photo, artist*

John Rais. Laying out the elements, marking the finials, and tweaking them for placement over the drawing. *Courtesy, artist*

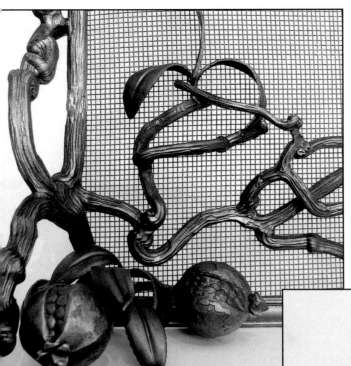

The pomegranate theme is one that Eric Clausen used throughout a private residence. The organic forms extend beyond the frame of the screen and become beautifully designed supports. Clausen has the experience, techniques, and design capabilities for twisting and shaping the hot iron into gnarled branches and graceful tendrils, and then texturing them so they represent the natural forms. Splitting the ripened fruits to show the seeds adds design, texture, and visual interest. The frame shape has an Art Nouveau inheritance, a design inspiration that Clausen explores often in his work.

Eric Clausen. Detail of Pomegranate Screen. The pomegranate branches were cleverly designed to become the base supports for the screen. *Photo, artist*

Eric Clausen. Free standing fire screen with pomegranates. The screen, made especially for this book, uses a theme developed for a client's private residence. *Photo, artist*

Clausen's floral screen with branches and leaves has a woven bottom that represents a fence. The woven area looks difficult to create in metal, but it is relatively simple, explained Clausen. A series of bends and loops are made for the "warp". Then each end is bent and the bent end is inserted into the weft at different heights. The leaves extend beyond the frame and into the branch that becomes the foot support.

Eric Clausen. Floral screen with woven steel elements in the Art Nouveau style. The branch extends down to form the foot support. *Photo, artist*

Eric Clausen. Detail of the woven elements executed in iron by bending the horizontal elements at regularly spaced intervals and then inserting the vertical bars that alternate in height. *Photo, artist*

Michael Bendele. One of the two free-standing fire
screens made for each end of the Toledo, Ohio, Metro
Parks Visitor Center. The design of the oposite screen
varies but is related. Each is asymmetrical. 28" high, 44"
wide, 14" deep. *Photo, Jim King*

Dimitri Gerakaris' plant forms entwine within the frame of the
fireplace doors. He coordinates the grate with the exterior frame
of the doors so that when the doors are open, the fireplace is a
unified visual statement. These pieces were made in the Adirondack
style to simulate the tree and twig forms associated with the area.

Dimitri Gerakaris. One of five fire doors for a residence built in the
Adirondack style with an organic motif. This one, for a large screened
porch, required special security locks to be integrated into the design.
Photo, artist

Dimitri Gerakaris. A matching log grate was designed using the same gutsy floral elements, as in his Adirondack style doors on page 45. *Photo, artist*

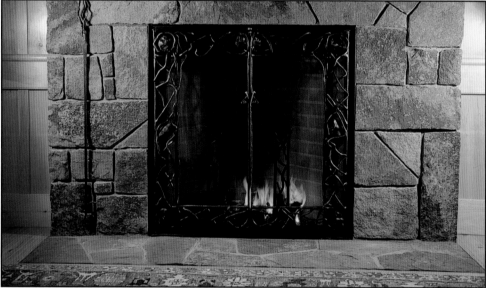

Dimitri Gerakaris. Double gated fire doors and fire tools designed and built in the Adirondack "twig work style." Gerakaris coordinated their design to complement the stonework and adjacent carpeting. *Photo, artist*

Oak trees with the leaves, acorns, and squirrels that feed upon them are popular subjects for the artist blacksmith. They can be a few simple branches as in Jeff Fetty's screen or they can be a whole story of the oak tree as in Glenn F. Gilmore's composition. Gilmore's screens have so much going on with finite attention to details. Studying them is like poring over a fine oil painting to see what the artist included and how he developed them. (See page 52.)

Michael Bondi's repoussé trees at the bottom sides of a tri-fold screen represent Japanese bonsai trees.

Jeff Fetty. Fire doors with oak leaves and an asymmetrical
top frame. *Photo, artist*

Opposite page: Michael Bondi. Forged and fabricated
folding fireplace screen with repoussé copper panels.
The raised repoussé panels are patterned after a bonsai
plant. Matching andirons. *Photo, Colin McCrae*

Corrina R. Mensoff. Fire screen with fern and hosta plants, a dragonfly, and butterfly. Collection Dick and Judy Allison. *Photo, Jill Buckner*

Photo of ferns and hosta that inspired Mensoff's fire screen.

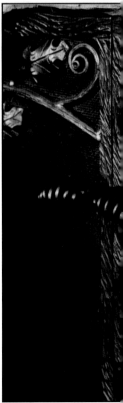

Glenn F. Gilmore. Detail of grape leaves and branches fire doors. Chiseled and formed texture suggests tree bark. The leaves and tendrils curl and the door latch, representing plant tendrils, houses a spring-loaded lever. *Photo, McNabb Studio*

Glenn F. Gilmore. Grape leaves and branches in a fire door set in mild steel with stainless steel mesh screen. A branch shape becomes the shaft for the matching tool set and the rim for the base plate. Doors are 36" x 36". Hearth tool set is 36" high. *Photo, McNabb Studio*

49

Glenn F. Gilmore. A great room fireplace with sea oats motifs. The fireplace doors have a textured frame with sea oats and the grate has related sea oats and leaf blades. The tool stand resembles a sand dune base with sea oats. Textured branches hold the tools. *Photo, McNabb Studio*

Keith Johnson's subject of squirrels eating acorns shows his ability to replicate the texture of the squirrel's fur and veins in the oak leaves. Richard Prazen's tree fills the full frame of the fireplace with an oak brush tree design. Carl Glowienke's (Sea Life Studio) fire doors with trees looks like a forest burning when the fire is lit.

Richard Glowienke (Sealife Sculpture Studio). Bronze screen with trees. When the fire behind the screen is lit, it looks like a forest burning. *Courtesy, artist*

Richard Prazen. Oak brush tree removable screen. The tree trunk at the screen bottom sends its branches and leaves across the screen. Additional leaf shapes are worked into the bottom frame that is earth-like in its shape. *Courtesy, artist*

Keith R. Johnson and Roger Loyson. Oak tree and squirrel fire doors. Steel doors and frame by Roger Loyson, bronze squirrel and oak leaves by Keith Johnson. Design by Architectural Impressions and Robert Walsh. *Photo, courtesy, Architectural Impressions*

Keith R. Johnson and Roger Loyson. Detail of oak tree and squirrel fire doors. The bronze squirrel nibbles at an acorn from the oak tree. A 1-inch mesh screen is used for the gas-burning fireplace. Wood burning fireplaces require a smaller mesh screen. *Photo, David Grondin*

In Gilmore's screen with oak leaves and acorns he has made the short branches part of the doorframe. Some have hollow ends and the others appear to have bark growing over the end, as would real trees. A few knotholes are included. The tool stand shaft is a textured branch, the tool handles have acorn tops, and the handle section is bark. Acorn stems become the tool holders. Leaves and acorns are highlighted with a brass brush finish.

Glenn F. Gilmore. Oak leaf and acorn fireplace doors and matching tool set. *Photo, McNabb Studio*

an F. Gilmore. Oak leaf and acorn fireplace door detail with "iron" knotholes evident. All pieces, ...ding the hearth tools, log grate, and hinges were forged in-house; no parts were purchased ... suppliers. *Photo, McNabb Studio*

It takes patience, time, and experience to forge and fabricate a scene such as the one Roland Greefkes made for actress Bette Midler. It's hard enough to make the objects and texture the frame, but chiseling out the lettering across the top is a major assignment. Each letter was chiseled and cut separately and a lot of filing and cold ironwork were required. Then the letters were welded in place from the back side of the frame.

The words, "And now the purple dust of twilight time steals across the meadow of my heart" are from Midler's favorite song. Said Greefkes, "Unfortunately, these words were her second choice; her first choice, 'Mehr Licht' meaning 'More Light' that she interpreted as 'More insight' was abandoned in favor of the much longer sentence that involved much more work." The owl at the top has special significance for the client. The trees and reindeer at the bottom suggest the winter scene.

Roland C. Greefkes. Bette Midler screen of wrought iron. Freestanding three panel folding screen has many subtle details that form the composition. An owl perches at the top left; an elk at bottom right appears to be looking back over his shoulder at the fir trees. A bird nestles among the tree leaves. 36" high, 66" wide. *Courtesy, artist*

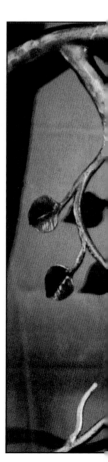

Roland C. Greefkes. Detail of the Bette Midler screen shows hand chiseled lettering across the top of the frame that reads, "Now the purple dust of twilight time steals across the meadow of my heart," is a line from Ms. Midler's favorite song. The 7-inch high wise owl oversees the scene. *Courtesy, artist*

When Bruce W. Brown was asked to design fireplace doors for a home in the Colorado Mountains, he sat down in front of the empty hearth trying to get a sense of what would work well. He said, "I looked around and to the right was a window with an arched top and an aspen tree growing outside." Why not bring the outside in, he thought, and then he decided to extend the branches beyond the fireplace opening. He also incorporated the hinges and latch into the branches so it would be as naturalistic as the tree.

Bruce W. Brown. Aspen tree fire doors inspired by a stand of trees outside the client's windows. *Photo, artist*

Bruce W. Brown. Detail of aspen tree and branches. *Photo, artist*

55

Bruce W. Brown. These doors are for a large fireplace in a master bedroom. The detailing ties in with a massive hand carved wooden headboard with vines and leaves. *Photo, artist*

Brown's lighter weight set of fireplace doors is in the master bedroom of the same house as the aspen doors. They pick up a design in a large hand carved wooden headboard. "The metal actually has a lighter look than the massive headboard purposely to lighten the feel of the two pieces in the same room," explained Brown.

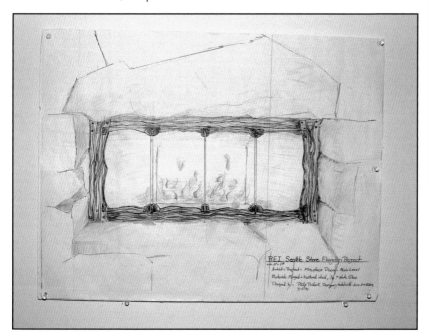

Phillip Baldwin. REI fireplace doors. Concept drawing for the doors focused on the ruggedness of the fireplace that is in the central area of the store. *Photo, artist*

Phillip Baldwin. REI fireplace doors captured the motif of weathered wood. The metallic textured surface forms a transition from the blocky stone to the fluidity of fire. *Photo, artist*

Phillip Baldwin. REI fireplace doors. Frame detail repeats the ruggedness and irregularity of the stone and relates to additional bars above the fireplace. Heavy bosses, suggestive of shells or fungus, form the hinges and catch elements of the door. *Photo, artist*

Animals, Fish, and Fowl Designs

Glenn F. Gilmore has earned a deserved reputation for his fire screens and fire tool hardware. His screens combine artistic design with forged, fabricated accessories that are hand fitted to the individual opening. That requires working on site. He hand forges the hinges, levers, and handles, and finishes them with his special mix of oil and paste wax. In addition to his meticulous workmanship, each of his screens is customized to accommodate a client's interests and visual ideas. He said, "Each screen (along with the hearth tools, log grate, and andirons) is designed to enhance the overall ambiance of the room, thus changing the fireplace area into a 'small gallery of art' to be enjoyed whether or not a fire is burning."

Gilmore's animal screen and tool set is like a trip through a forest where elk reside among the fir trees. The elk, fir trees, and the ground were shaped with a plasma cutting tool that made it easy to achieve the jagged edges on the trees. The shapes were left flat rather than rounded out. Animal heads became the fire tool handles.

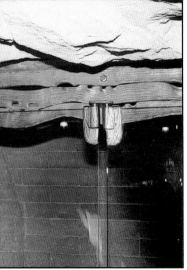

Phillip Baldwin, who favors outdoors activities, was pleased when the architects for REI, a store that sells equipment for outdoor living, asked him to create a firescreen for their flagship store in Seattle, Washington. Baldwin said, "During the review of the architectural goals, perusal of renderings, and touring the site, I sensed the attempt to communicate and encourage the 'authentic experience.'" The building is very physical. To enter, you walk through a sensory laden landscape. Rough, honest materials are used on the scale one associates with the high Cascade Mountains. The fireplace is in the center of the store. It is big, rough, a veritable mini-mountain with fire in its belly at least part of the year. The idea was to create an effect that was naturalistic, had an informal solidity, and was very much in keeping with the fireplace and the building as a whole."

Glenn F. Gilmore. Detail of fireplace doors with elk and fir trees. Trees and elk were plasma cut from 14-gauge sheet metal. Color is acquired by heating the metals to different temperatures, and then finished with a mixture of oil and paste wax rubbed in. *Photo, McNabb Studio*

It's easy to see Jerry A. Coe's affection for Art Nouveau and its influences on his fire screens. None are perfect squares or rectangles. Rather they are curving, graceful shapes with linear elements that suggest movement and flow. He favors forged bronze because of its feel and warm colors. Animal shapes may be made first in clay, then cast in bronze.

Jerry A. Coe. Forged bronze freestanding screen with bird family. Post Art Nouveau style. Private residence, Cape Cod, Massachusetts. *Photo, artist*

Jerry A. Coe. Detail of birds that have been forged. *Photo, artist*

Opposite page: Glenn F. Gilmore. Fireplace doors with elk and fir trees have twist handles that are matched in the fire tool set. The tool set has a tripod stand with the client's ranch brand on the top with horse head handles. Cloud and mountain silhouettes carry through the linear elements in the marble surround. *Photo, McNabb Studio*

Jerry A. Coe. Fire screen in forged bronze with cast and forged animals. Art Nouveau style. Private residence in St. Helena, California. *Photo, artist*

Jerry A. Coe. Detail of the rabbit first created in clay, then cast in bronze. *Photo, artist*

Jerry A. Coe. Detail of the turtle first made in clay, then cast in bronze. *Photo, artist*

Jerry A. Coe. Free standing shaped fire screen with willows and a mouse. Forged bronze. *Photo, artist*

Jerry A. Coe. Detail of mouse with a pocket watch. *Photo, artist*

Jerry A. Coe. French provincial freestanding screen with birds and leaves. Private residence in St. Helena, California. *Photo, Richard Sargent*

Kirk Sullens with Michael Robinson from a concept drawing by John Perkins. Sullens' steel repoussé figures were worked with handmade tools recycled from old tools. The figures are less than 1/4" thick but give the feeling of deep perspective. *Photo, Chris Gray*

Kirk Sullen's repoussé horse and rider capture action when lassoing the running bull. Achieving the feeling of action and perspective in three dimensional space in less than 1/4-inch depth requires technical virtuosity. The cowboy's arm crosses the door opening so the break is at the hand holding the lariat. "When a client brought in a picture of a cowboy and horse scene, we changed it to cowboys and cattle, worked it in three dimensions, and this is the result. It was fun and creative to do," said Sullens.

Robert E. Wiederrick. Buffalo Hunt fire screen with arrowhead handles. Hammer textured mild steel with a natural brushed finish. *Photo, artist*

Robert Wiederrick's inventive themes of nature for fireplace doors and screens are so varied that viewing an assortment of them is like looking at a one-man show. His variety and versatility are refreshing, often humorous, as in the screen with the beaver nibbling at the doorframe. "Often, I am inventing and trying new things as I go as in the screen with the bear," said Wiederrick. "It was my first attempt at a high relief animal form. I built up the shape by MIG welding pieces to the head and arms. To simulate fur texture, I used a cut-off wheel on a grinding tool. For texture on a trout, I sand blasted over a piece of the screening."

Robert E. Wiederrick. California Quail fire screen. The client liked quail and wanted a scene that would represent a quail family. Hammer texture with a natural brushed finish. 42" high, 61" wide. *Photo, artist*

Wiederrick, whose shop is constantly busy, says that word of mouth accounts for most of his clients. He lives in a mountain resort community around Sun Valley, Idaho, where skiing is popular and the fireplace is always a focal point of après-ski socializing. His clients inevitably want a theme screen that will illustrate their interests, or their views of the surrounding areas. He enjoys the challenge of developing a scene with animals, people, plants, and environments portrayed on them.

Robert E. Wiederrick. A beaver chomps at the tree trunk that is the fire door frame textured to look like a tree. *Photo, artist*

Robert E. Wiederrick. A combination of studying a drawing of a real beaver and a cartoon beaver resulted in this image. It has a chiseled fur texture. *Photo, artist*

Robert E. Wiederrick. "Flying Ducks" fire doors were inspired by the wild life on a nearby silver creek nature preserve. Cattails are made of forged pipe. Hammer textured steel with a brown patina finish. 41" high, 50" wide. *Photo, artist*

Robert E. Wiederrick. A duck with chiseled details, attached to the screen mesh, appears to be flying. Sheet steel with brown patina finish. *Photo, artist*

Robert E. Wiederrick. "End of the Trail" has a single arrowhead handle at the side of the one panel screen. Hammer textured steel with a natural brushed finish. 31" high, 44" wide. *Photo, artist*

Robert E. Wiederrick. End of the Trail rider. Details are chiseled on IOGA plate steel. Hammer texture with a natural brushed finish. The detail illustrates different surface texture on three elements of the door's frame, the horse, and the retired rider's garment. *Photo, artist*

Robert E. Wiederrick. The high relief image of the bear was created with MIG welding to build out the head and arms. A small cut-off wheel was used to simulate the fur texture. *Photo, artist*

Robert E. Wiederrick. A snow scene with a bear among narrow, stately pine trees *Photo, artist*

Joe Miller. Fire screen with squirrels climbing up onto the oak tree that spans the screen's surface. *Photo, artist*

Joe Miller. The finely shaped and detailed squirrel is graceful and lifelike; quite an achievement when rendered in iron. *Photo, artist*

Joe Miller. Fire screen is a landscape. Though only two dimensional, the clever use of lines gives it a three-dimensional appearance. A bird is perched on the tree trunk at left, and rabbit peers from the bushes, below right. The composition uses the space at the screen's sides so there is a clear view of the fire. *Photo, artist*

Joe Miller. A bird, perched on the tree trunk is so lifelike; you can almost hear it chirping along with the crackle of the fire. *Photo, artist*

Joe Miller. The rabbit seems to have his jaws filled with acorns from the tree. *Photo, artist*

John Rais. Preying Mantis fire screen. Forged steel, patina, and paint. 40" high, 60" wide, 16" deep. The design captures the mantis' habitat among reeds and other mantes. *Photo, artist*

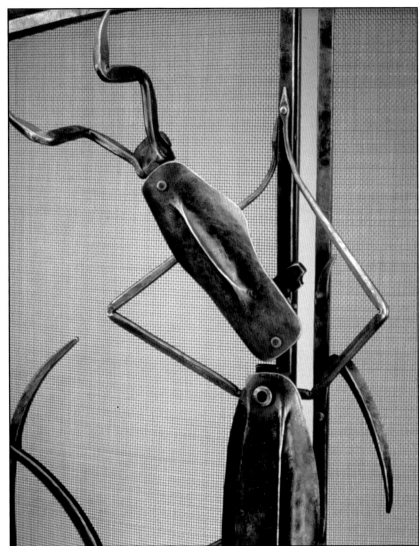

John Rais. Detail of mantis that is the handle for opening and closing the doors. *Photo, artist*

Glenn F. Gilmore. Freestanding fire screen showing three deer crossing the plain. Pine tree branches and pinecones above help create a scene. Deer were made from sheet metal, then shaped by forging to give them a 3-dimensional appearance. The tool set has forged horse heads on the top and graceful twisted handles. Doors are 40" high, 60" wide. *Photo, McNabb Studio*

Glenn F. Gilmore. Detail of branch and deer. *Photo, McNabb Studio*

Robert E. Wiederrick. Trout fire doors inspired by the client who is an avid fly fisher. Single panel door with a hammer texture and a brown patina finish. 36" high, 39" wide. *Photo, artist*

Robert E. Wiederrick. Trout catching the fly. Trout has chiseled details; the "scales" were sand blasted through the screen mesh to achieve the pattern. Steel with a brown patina finish. *Photo, artist*

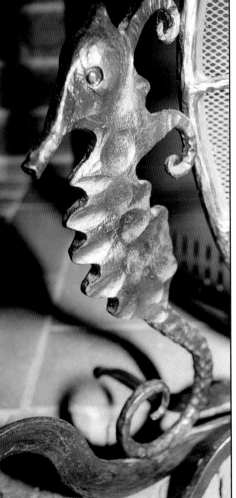

Australian blacksmith, Boyd P. Thompson, designed this screen to bring the sea indoors in a land locked Australian home. It also keeps children's hands away from the very hot glass in front of the fire. The wall sculpture of Australian Gum leaves reflects the eucalyptus forest nearby and complements the fire tools with handles that simulate the leaves of the Australian gum tree.

Boyd P. Thompson. Detail of the seahorse. *Photo, artist*

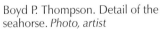

Boyd P. Thompson. The motif for this fire screen is a large, stylized representation of a nautilus shell being towed across the sea by a seahorse. Fire tools hang at right on an antique wall sculpture. *Photo, artist*

71

Glenn F. Gilmore. Freestanding fire screen with a silhouetted abstract seashell design flanked by forged seahorses. The tripod stand holds tools with twisted round stock handles. *Photo, McNabb Studio*

E. A. Chase. Fire doors and tools with Mayan motifs. *Photo, artist*

Glenn F. Gilmore. Shrimp boat scene represents the area along the coast of South Carolina where the client lives. There are a bronze shrimp net and a bronze wave. *Photo, McNabb Studio*

Glenn F. Gilmore. Detail of shrimp boat shows the fish shaped handle at left. Bar ends of the grate are fish tails. The screen, grate, and tools are Monel 400 metal, a non-corrosive material made from nickel and copper that resists rust and deterioration from ocean saltwater. *Photo, McNabb Studio*

Opposite page: Jerry A. Coe. Fire screen forged and hand sewn. Bronze and copper. The design, based on a Yosemite Indian basket pattern, has bronze feathers on each side. For a private residence in San Francisco, California. *Photo, Richard Sargent*

Non-objective and Objective Designs

Each artist finds inspiration for his work in past historical ideas, in nature, and in a variety of other sources. Sometimes they are combined in one project. This section focuses on designs for accessories that spring from the artist's imagination, use of geometric shapes, scrolls, curves, details, symbolism, and objects. Subjects are infinite and as varied as are the artists themselves.

Some artist's designs have distinctively recognizable styles. Their work may reflect repeat motifs, details, and elements just as Picasso's canvases are uniquely Picasso's. You may discover individualized design threads in the works of many of the artist blacksmiths. In time, each person's work may become as individually valued as masters in other media. Still others can be as versatile as the client and commission demand. They can easily move from a classical to a very contemporary style, from a busy, ornate statement to one that is simple and understated.

As you view the examples and their details keep in mind the perception of steel and its hardness that suggest a seeming intractability that would hinder its versatility. However, this intractability changes when it is subjected to heat; then infinite shaping potential is inherent in the medium. The material is probably more versatile, durable, and longer lasting than most other media. It doesn't break when dropped, as does ceramics, it doesn't deteriorate or burn as does wood. It will deteriorate if exposed to weathering and moisture but that can take ages. It can be made as malleable as clay when it is heated; and formed into shapes not possible with clay. It can emulate textures and shapes of wood. It is stronger and longer lasting than either clay or wood, and it doesn't burn. If you think of steel mainly as a building material, now's the time to alter that thinking and recognize its practicality as a viable medium for artistic functional objects.

Frederic A. Crist and David W. Munn. Campbell/ Goetz fireplace doors, tools, and andirons designed to function with a Rumford fireplace. The doors are set on roller bearings and hung on a decorative angle to slide out to the side when in use and to close at night and cut off the draft. *Photo, Frederic A. Crist*

Geometric and Imaginary Designs

Frederic A. Crist and David W. Munn have an unending variety of design concepts in their large body of work. Their Campbell/Goetz firescreen and Leigh fireplace doors are designed with hard line, geometric elements. A freestanding fire screen echoes the antique Italian headboard that is whimsical and traditional. They seem to have fun drawing out the ends of the iron in gravity defying squiggles. Both the screen and the headboard are used in one room and could only be coordinated with a custom design. It also illustrates how deft and clever early Italian ironmongers were in combining wood and iron.

The Mayan tiles in the Art Deco fireplace at the Winters House of the Bellevue Historical Society, Bellevue, Washington, suggested the design for Russell Jaqua's beautifully rendered firescreen with flat bars as the frame. The corner stepped elements are typical of Mayan architectural elements.

Russell Jaqua. Winter's House fire screen was designed to complement the stepped shape of the hearth and its magnificent Mayan motif tiles. The simple, but bold, geometric pattern in the screen's corners was accomplished with a Nazel power hammer. *Photo, Robert Gibeau*

These designs formed the basis of many of the geometric motifs in Art Deco designs. The discovery of the Mayan architecture in the early 1920s inspired artists of the era to replicate the forms that appealed to them, and that inspiration continues among today's artists.

Flat iron bars are also the basis of Christopher Thomson's fire screen with S-scrolls and a stylized plant form in the center. Coiled handles at the top are used to move the freestanding screen. Rivets are both functional and decorative.

Christopher Thomson. A flat frame freestanding fire screen with geometric corners, S-scrolls along the bottom, and a stylized leaf form in the center. Bronze rivets are used for function, contrast, and design. *Photo, Susan Livermore*

It's easy to detect the inspiration for artwork containing nature's objects such as trees and animals. But other inspirations can be subtler, even obtuse, unless they're pointed out. James Viste's unusual detailing on the frame and interior elements in his fire doors take their cue from an African mask in the client's mask collection. The client wanted the fire screen to reflect detailing that natives carved in wood. Could Viste do in metal what African carvers did in wood? Of course. The result is stunning and different.

Frederic A. Crist and David W. Munn. Leigh fire doors were made to match a set of Art Nouveau style railings in the same house. Hand polished and finished with polyurethane. The doors swing open far enough for access to the equipment for adjusting the gas log flame. *Photo, Frederic A. Crist*

Frederic A. Crist and David W. Munn. Summer fire screen is shown with a wood and iron antique headboard that it complements. The headboard was originally the back of an Italian wedding cart and the fire screen complements it. A summer fire screen is a decorative cover for the hearth opening during seasons when the fire is not lit. *Photo, Frederic A. Crist*

James Viste. The owner of several African artifacts commissioned the fire doors. The African mask was the inspiration for the artist blacksmith's use of the notched motif in metal for a modern home in Grosse Point Park, Michigan. Collection, John Korachis. *Photo, artist*

James Viste. The African mask that inspired the fire doors has a zigzag notch-like motif that Viste captured in iron. *Photo, artist*

E. A. Chase. A freestanding fireplace screen is in the Tudor style. Tudor period fireplaces had restrained ornamentation, but they featured medallions and a coat of arms. *Photo, artist*

A "Tudor" style is one of many fireplace screens by E. A. Chase, whose design versatility is awesome. Chase has a deep rooted knowledge of art history that he combines with exacting craftsmanship. He mixes various metals for color, interest, and durability. He may combine iron, copper, brass, aluminum, and Chrome-Moly steel in a screen and tools. His handles and hinges are invariably jewel-like.

David Tuthill's project of a firescreen and surround (or facing) for a remodeled home proved a challenging project, said the artist. It required working with a series of patterns, and a stonemason. The outer frame and copper were riveted together, and then every third rivet was omitted. He then threaded these rivets and hand tightened each one as it was mounted to the armature behind the frame. For the chain mail screen, an assistant patiently assembled the 4,000 plus links together to complete the screen. Tuthill also made the matching fire tools.

Corrina R. Mensoff's design for the fire door featuring the Mongolian Symbol for Eternal Hearth evolved from a series of conversations and drawings between the client, Vanessa Vadim, and the artist. The inspiration came from an original etching by the client with imagery important to her that related to the hearth of her home. The crescent moon and sun are symbolic of early nature religion, prior to Buddhism. The three flames rising from the sun/moon represent the past, present, and future...the hearth being a place to gather for friends and family. Mensoff notes, "I took into consideration the aesthetics of the Arts & Crafts period home, in harmony with the symbolism, and spiritual harmony of the client's ideas.

Corrina R. Mensoff. The presentation drawing for the Mongolian Symbol fireplace doors.

David Tuthill. Screen, surround or facing, proved a challenging job because the elements had to be worked into the arch design. The mild steel and copper fire screen was for a remodeled home; another fireplace on the floor above shared the same chimney. The screen is composed of 4,000 hand linked chain mail links. *Photo, Jay Dotson*

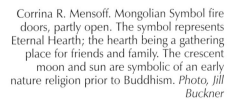

Corrina R. Mensoff. Mongolian Symbol fire doors, partly open. The symbol represents Eternal Hearth; the hearth being a gathering place for friends and family. The crescent moon and sun are symbolic of an early nature religion prior to Buddhism. *Photo, Jill Buckner*

"It's a positive feeling to create harmony between aesthetic beauty, utilitarian function, and spiritual significance…this fireplace seems to come alive with the warm flames glowing in the background! The Old World meets the new in ancient symbolism mixed with today's technology and environment."

Another of Mensoff's commissions required the cooperative talents of four artists whose combined talents created this incredibly beautiful and complex corner fireplace treatment for a renovated house in the Arts & Crafts style. The wall and hearth were designed by Charlie Smith, and the mantel by David Kreglowski. The screen and tools of forged iron and naval brass were made by Mensoff with the assistance of Bo Weaver. Says Mensoff, "I used different colors of metal like checkers, bouncing color off each other; the yellow of the brass onto steel and the dark steel back onto the brass. The screen was made to go around a corner opening with two hinges and attached to the hearth and mantel to pivot. The client wanted the look of the entire area to be contemporary, masculine, and geometric. It was a refreshing design and working on the project was a joy."

Corrina R. Mensoff, Bo Weaver, Charlie Smith, and David Kreglowski. Lazarus corner fireplace screens. The fireplace was a collaboration between four artists. The forged iron and naval brass screen, wood box, and tools were designed by Corrina Mensoff, and made by Mensoff and Bo Weaver. The wall and hearth were made by Charlie Smith, and the mantel by David Kreglowski. The unit was designed to fit into a contemporary renovation of an Arts & Crafts period home. *Photo, Jill Buckner*

Corrina R. Mensoff. Detail of the Mongolian Symbol fire doors shows the texture, colors, and shapes of the iron. Note that the artist signed the piece. *Photo, Jill Buckner*

John Boyd Smith also solved the problem of a wrap around fireplace for an Arts & Crafts style house. He forged three separate screens of textured iron with copper bars along the top and copper rivets. The matching tool set repeats the copper rivet detailing; all have irregularly forged heads for detail interest.

John Boyd Smith. Another solution for a wrap around fire screen is a tri-fold Arts & Crafts style matched screen and tool set of forged steel with copper rivets. The hearth and fireplace are composed of cement with embedded oyster shells.
Photo, Rhonda Nell Fleming

Opposite page: John Boyd Smith. Detail of the tops of t
matched fire tools. The tools are long to match the scale of t
screen and fireplace. They must be carefully weighted so they c
be easily manipulated for tending the fire. Copper rivets provid
function, color and decoration. *Photo, Rhonda Nell Flemi*

Additional accessories by E. A. Chase are in different styles with an array of individualized details. They may combine several metals for color and texture contrasts; steel, stainless steel, brass, bronze, chrome, and copper.

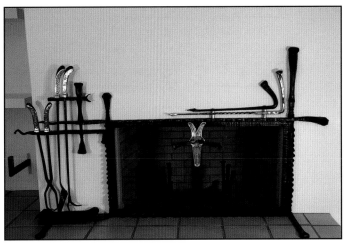

E. A. Chase. Fire screen and tools in combinations of iron, chrome, and brass. The exterior frame extends beyond the hearth opening in an asymmetrical arrangement. The tool holder is an extension of the top frame piece. *Photo, artist*

E. A. Chase. Three sided fire screen with two tool holders. One holder has the poker and shovel, the other has the broom and tongs. The corners of the screen repeat the shape of the fireplace corners. *Photo, artist*

E. A. Chase. Iron, brass, and copper fire screen with fleur-de-lis. The frame edge is grooved to match the grooving in the wooden fireplace front. *Photo, artist*

Dimitri Gerakaris' screens have an overall look of simplicity with subtle ornamentation such as elegant curves and tactilely inviting surface texturing. His bi-folding doors with stylized tree motif andirons form an artistic, sculptural composition when they are opened or closed.

Dimitri Gerakaris. A bi-folding screen with matching, stylized tree-motif andirons for the guesthouse of an Adirondack style home. In the open position the andirons provide the main decorative element. *Photo, artist*

Dimitri Gerakaris. Adirondack style doors in the closed position. The curve of the frame top and the curves in the andirons form a unifying composition. *Photo, artist*

Geometric shapes in varying relationships help simplify a design when cleverly used. Often they are interspersed with C-scrolls, a basic element in blacksmithing, as in John Phillips' Lake House fire doors. The composition consists of a circle with horizontal and vertical members softened by splitting and making a C-scroll at the ends of two of the bars.

John Phillips. Lake House fire doors so called because they are installed the lake house of a client. Lines, a central circle, an arced frame, and repeat C-scrolls are combined in an arrangement that lends a strict geometry as a contrast to the random complex patterning in the stone fireplace itself. *Photo, artist*

Jim Wallace's "Pontius" freestanding screen subtly gives the effect of Indian artifacts in the arrow shape above the fireplace and the feather like pieces within. The matching andirons, see page 165, carry out the theme.

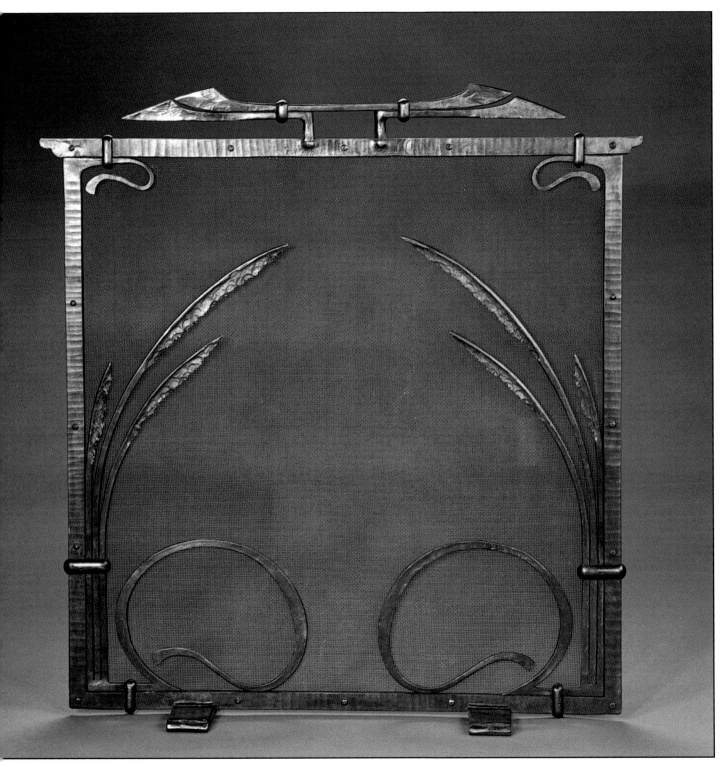

Jim Wallace. Pontius Fireplace Screen is elegant in its simplicity, repeat use of curves, the unusual handle at the top, and the exquisite surface texturing. Mild steel. 39" high, 38" wide. *Photo, Murray Ris*

Nicholas Such subscribes to the theory that "less is more" in the screen that uses only geometric shapes resulting in a fool-the-eye perspective.

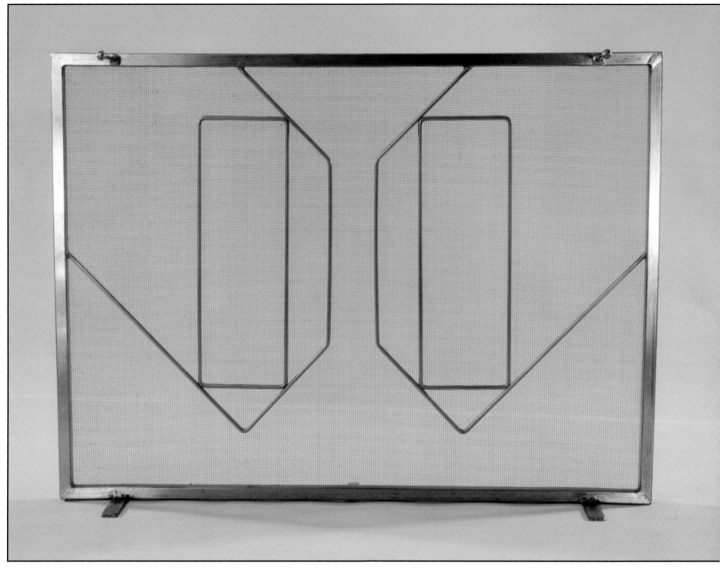

Nicholas Such. A geometric minimalist design with perspective in a freestanding fire screen. Made of welded steel, chrome steel, with galvanized wire cloth. The frame is polished and finished with a clear lacquer. 25" high, 36" wide, 1" deep.
Photo, Paul Moshay

The importance of details to Andrew Macdonald is apparent in his traditionally designed screen for a client in Virginia. To him, the backside of the screen is as important as the front. The hand forged hinges have no exposed welds, and the back frame with angle iron is 1/4" narrower than the front frame. With this technique, he sandwiched the wire cloth between the frames, and then riveted the frames together so that the screen edges are hidden as you look down the screen. This is a more time consuming procedure, but aesthetically more pleasing than having the raw edges of the screening exposed. Additionally, the rivets provide a repeat decorative element.

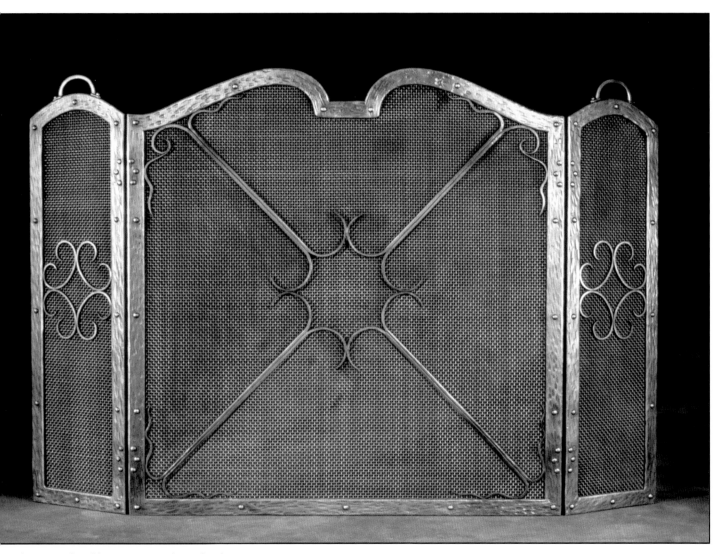

Andrew Macdonald. Even in a traditional style screen, curves in the frame top, simple lines and basic C-scrolls can result in a unique statement. This three part freestanding screen was for the addition to a log cabin house in Virginia. The textured frame, placement of the rivets around the frame, and hinges, add to the design.
Photo, Jeffery Bruce

Steve Lopes. Simplicity and rivet details are also present in this Craftsman style screen. The frame is steel with contrasting bronze rivets and handle. *Photo, artist*

Jim Gallucci. Humor in a functional object like a fire screen is rare but Gallucci captures the essence of the spider web and its maker in this delightfully conceived screen with simple straight lines. The tri-fold screen is aptly named, "The Spider Web" screen. *Photo, David Brown*

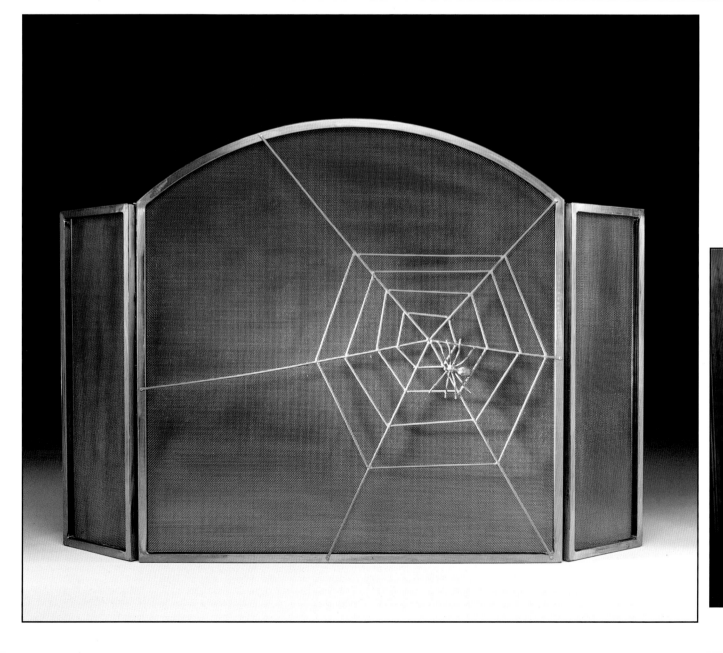

Stephen Bondi. One of four fireplace accessory sets for a private residence in Alamo, California. This one for the formal living area is curved with arches on the doors. A frame of twisted square bar is riveted to each panel. The copper and green colors are intended to be reminiscent of the Art Nouveau, and Art Deco work of the Italian blacksmith, Carlo Rizzarda. 32" high, 48" wide, 12" deep. *Photo, Stephen Bondi* © Bondi Metals

Robert E. Wiederrick. The handles of the doors were inspired by curved details in the mantel. The screen required unique construction because there was no top framework for securing the latch to the doors. *Photo, artist*

Robert E. Wiederrick. A 17th century classic fireplace imported from Lyon, France, calls for a classic treatment but it needn't be as ornate as the fireplace. It was deemed wiser to keep the fire doors simple and elegant. The result is a screen that follows the curve of the mantel and is textured to pick up the visual veining of the marble. *Photo, artist*

Dan Nauman. C-scrolls repeated in different sizes within, and also protruding into a third dimension satisfied the clients request for a screen with classic lines that wasn't "too busy." The scrolls and acanthus leaves are classic elements. Depressions in the frame were made with various sizes of ball peen hammers. Mild steel. 40" high, 50" wide. *Photo, George Lottermoser*

Dan Nauman. Detail of classic screen shows the craftsmanship in the beautifully forged scrolls, the anthemion, and the peening. *Photo, George Lottermoser*

Craig Kaviar. Tri-fold screen has curved handles. The design is
repeated on each panel of the screen. *Photo, artist*

Jeff Fetty and James Horrobin use diamond patterns but in very different arrangements.

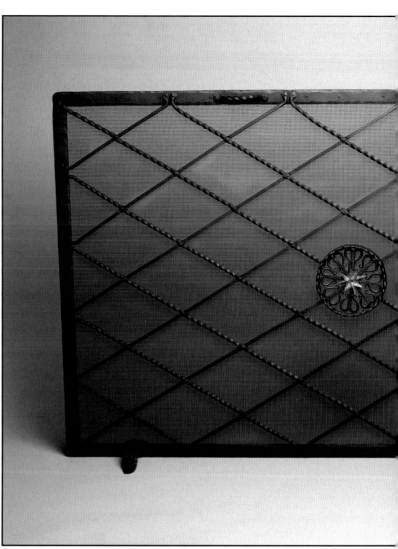

Jeff Fetty. A diamond arrangement with alternating textured and plain bars gives the screen a changing visual perspective from a flat plane to a three dimensional appearance. The circular medallion in the center is the focal point. Forged steel and brass. 33" high, 42" wide. *Photo, Michael Keller*

James Horrobin. Fire screen 2. Scrolls and oval shapes with leaves exhibit an intricate repeat design that is both traditional and modern. *Photo, artist*

James Horrobin. A four part folding screen with angled squares. The ends of each square element evolve into a graceful curve that softens the geometry of the straight lines. *Photo, artist*

Christopher Thomson. A patterned woven screening is used rather than traditional square mesh, and makes this three-part freestanding screen unusual. *Photo Susan Livermore*

Jefferson Mack. A steel fire screen with bronze rivets. The circular topped black andirons provide relief from the starkness of the stone wall and the hanging steel mantel. *Photo, Tom MacAffee*

Chris Axelsson. The simplicity of this freestanding screen, a perfect accompaniment to a Craftsman style fireplace mantle, belies the complexity of the design. The frame's straight lines and curves hold screening molded and bent to form the brass horizontal and vertical bands that help hold the shape. The andirons, with the same bands as the screen, contribute to its harmony. *Photo, artist*

Jerry A. Coe's design for the bronze fire doors has the understated designs from a Japanese basket as its theme. The tools hang on a stand that fits to the wall. The top bracket is attached to the fireplace but protrudes far enough from the wall so the tool handles will hook on. A brush, rather than a broom, is attached to a forged shank with a curved edge.

Jerry A. Coe. Fire screen and fire tool set based on a design from a Japanese basket. Forged bronze. Subtle, exquisite detailing lend elegance to the screen. Note the screen and tool handles and the twist on the shaped brush handle. *Photo, artist*

Bruce W. Brown's fireplaces usually pose an inordinate construction challenge and interesting problems to solve. A double-sided fireplace was made of the roughest rock he ever had to work with. There were beautiful Persian rugs and ornate furniture that gave him reason to create ornate hinges. The see-through unit meant designing doors for each side of the fireplace, doubling the problems.

Bruce W. Brown. Fireplace set with andirons. The knobs on the bottom of the doors are for air intake as the fireplace has no outside air feed. The andirons were made from a pair of horse hitching posts. *Photo, artist*

Opposite page, top: Bruce W. Brown. The same fireplace doors closed. The hinges were simple so as not to detract from the andirons and gate. The grate has C-scroll ends on each bar. The beige patina ties in with color of the stones instead of using a black finish, *Photo, artist*

Bottom: Bruce W. Brown. Double sided fireplace with a slightly different screen on each side, see page 100. *Photo, artist*

Bruce W. Brown. This double-sided fireplace, see page 99, has this screen on the other side; you can see through the glass to the windows outside. *Photo, artist*

Objects As Designs

Specific objects, some real and some symbolic, stylized, or abstract, are targeted design subjects for many attractive and unique screens and doors.

Christopher Thomson. Snakelike squiggly shapes at the screen bottom of this kiva fireplace screen seem to emerge as licks of fire. The squiggles extend in front of the screen to form the supports The coiled handle design is repeated in the fire tool handles. *Photo, David Marlowe*

Stephen Bondi. Fireplace screen and tools. With carefully bent horizontals and verticals the screen appears to be woven. Some parts of the bars are flattened to give a random weaving effect, but they are anything but random. Each hammer blow, each section is carefully balanced to play against the surrounding sections. The matching tool set has the same texturing. *Photo, artist*

Daniel Miller. "Reliquary for the Angel of the Chestnut Forest" has symbolic references to chestnut leaves and branches that had been destroyed by blight. Collection, The Swag Hotel, Waynesville, North Carolina. *Photo, Weststar Photographic*

Daniel Miller says his fire doors, "Reliquary for the Angel of the Chestnut Forest," is the only screen he ever titled, probably because of guilt surrounding the demise of the Chestnut Forest in America destroyed by blight. Before the blight, one in every six hardwoods in America was chestnut. Shortly after the screen was commissioned for The Chestnut Room of The Swag Hotel in Waynesville, North Carolina, Miller took a trip to Italy where he observed church reliquaries with bones of saints displayed in beautiful gold, and glass and silver containers. The bones were usually secured in place with metal bands. "I worked on this screen an inordinately long time, not really knowing where I was going but ending up with two iron chestnut tree leaves and branches." said Miller. "Finally, when close to completion I looked at the screen across the shop and was shocked to see what appeared like the skeleton of an angel with the leaves as wings, and the branches as bones, secured in place for display with the same kind of metal bands I had seen in Italy."

Rod Pickett. Western style door with braided trim and concho details. Conchos are at the corners and used for the handles. Iron with a waxed rusted finish. 32" high, 55" wide. *Photo, Julie Pickett*

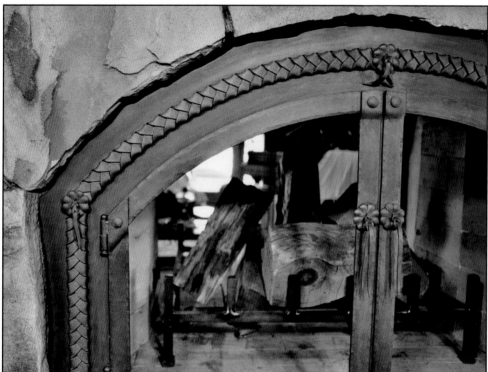

Rod Pickett. Details of the iron braid work and the conchos. Observe how carefully the frame must be fashioned to fit into the fireplace's stone at the corner and sides. *Photo, Julie Pickett*

Glenn F. Gilmore's Captain's Wheel fireplace doors and matching tool set is the focal point for a room with a nautical theme. Gilmore cleverly used the circle and handles as geometric elements. The round center plate is brass, the latch is naval bronze finished with a chocolate patina. Door handles at the top are twisted and looped for a square knot effect. The grate has two forged ships anchors as log rests. Stainless steel screen was used for its color contrast and durability.

Glenn F. Gilmore. Captain's wheel fire doors designed for a room with a nautical theme. Mild steel with brass rivets. The center plate is brass; the latch is naval bronze finished with a chocolate patina. *Photo, McNabb Studio*

Glenn F. Gilmore. Game room fire screen and tools with a sports theme. An autographed bat is the shaft for the tools, topped by an autographed baseball. Tool shafts are antique woods. *Photo, McNabb Studio*

In Gilmore's freestanding fire screen for a workout room, the handles at the top are barbells with steel forged arms and hands holding them to the frames. The screen supports are forged legs and feet. Three human figures along the path at the screen bottom are a diver, a runner, and a weight lifter. The client, from Atlanta, Georgia, is a fan of the Braves baseball team, hence the baseball bat used for the stand shaft. It is engraved with signatures of players from the Atlanta Braves and the New York Yankees World Series won by the Braves. Braves pitcher Tom Gavin signed the baseball on top. Gilmore used antique wood shafted golf clubs for the tools. The stand base is a barbell weight resting on golf ball feet.

Glenn F. Gilmore. Detail of the game room fire screen shows the runner's path along the bottom with the figures of a runner, weight lifter, and diver. *Photo, McNabb Studio*

John Boyd Smith. Arts & Craft style forged steel fire screen with glass inserts. The 2.5" thick cast polished glass is by glass artist Lauren Herter. *Photo, Rhonda Nell Fleming*

Texture and glass inserts are the dominating elements of John Boyd Smith's Arts & Crafts style firescreen for a private resident on one of Georgia's Coastal Islands. The deep, carefully controlled indents pick up lights and reflect colors from the fire. Rivets, hinges, and handles are all hand forged.

Chapter 4

Fireplace Tool Sets

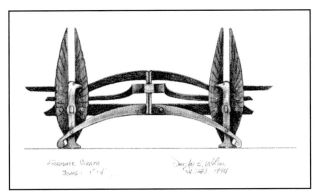

Douglas E. Wilson.
Sketch for a fireplace grate. *Courtesy, artist*

Fireplace tool sets may consist of a stand that holds a poker, a pair of tongs, a shovel, and a broom. These are necessary for wood burning fireplaces but not every set includes every tool. Fireplaces with gas logs may not require any tools but people often like them as a decorative accessory. The examples illustrate a variety of tools that could easily accompany any decorative style from Renaissance, to colonial, to contemporary. They are freestanding or wall hung and most are made of forged iron. Some combine iron with other materials such as deer antlers, horn, stone, wood, stainless steel, and Lucite. Often andirons and grates match the tool set.

Mass produced tool sets may be made by casting pieces from original shapes, then reproducing them and assembling the parts in a factory setting. The pieces are generally smooth, without the hand texturing of the custom-made one-of-a-kind tool set. They can still be very beautiful, but inevitably they lack the originality, surface texturing, and warmth of the handmade set. Some sets may be all cast iron.

Daniel Miller. Wedge Fire tool set. The shovel and poker fit over the horizontal bar; the tongs hang on the back of the bar. Mild steel.
Courtesy, Weststar Photographic

When you plan to buy fireplace tools here are factors to consider:

Should they match the screen or be a separate design entity? How high should they be? They should be scaled to the height of the fireplace and the firebox but still be easy to handle.

How are they hung in the holding device? Are they easy to remove and replace, and will they hold if they are bumped or moved?

How are the tool shafts attached to the tool itself? They may be riveted or forged all in one piece. Mass produced pieces may be secured only with screws and nuts that are less esthetic, less secure, and less expensive.

Can brooms or brushes be easily replaced if they become worn, dirty, or burned?

How heavy is the stock? Can you lift them and handle them easily or are they too heavy and ungainly? Be sure there are no sharp edges.

If the set will be wall hung, is the wall bracket easily mountable in stone, brick, or other material? Are the hanging devices strong enough to hold the tools?

If you want matching andirons and grates, are they available? Are they heavy enough so as not to belly under the heat of a fire?

The physical considerations of the tools are always foremost in the blacksmith's mind. How do they feel, how are they weighted? What is the scale of the tool to the fireplace and the screen? Tools can be made to coordinate with the fire doors or firescreen. Occasionally, a client will request a tool set with specific symbolism such as the baseball theme in Glenn Gilmore's tool set and screen, see page 106.

To appreciate what is involved in creating these tools it helps to understand the processes and techniques. Each tool begins with a length of plain round or flat iron bar in different diameters or thickness'. The iron is heated in a forge to make it malleable. Then, using hand or power tools, the artist can create myriad shapes and scrolls. The iron can be tied in a knot, looped, braided, and twisted. Twists are common and the types and sizes of twists can be as different as fingerprints. Some twists are tight, some loose, some in one direction, perhaps in two or three directions, and some appear braided; the variations possible are infinite.

L. Japheth Howard. One can easily appreciate the workmanship, detail, and evidence of strength, involved in creating the fireplace tool set in these two details from a set by a master blacksmith. Note the banding, the ends of the tools, and the surface texturing. *Photo, Jay Dotson*

Tool Stands

The tool stands, or holders, may be flat or footed with three or four feet for support. Often the tool and foot ends are upset and then shaped flat, rounded, forged into hexagonal or octagonal facets, or into a flower, a leaf, an animal head, and other objects. Ends may be decorated with brass, bronze, or other metals for color contrast. Sometimes, a faux finish is added to the steel so it appears to be the color of another metal.

Russell Jaqua believes that a well-crafted set of tools containing a poker, shovel, tongs, and broom handle requires the mastery of almost the whole range of traditional blacksmithing skills. In this sense, the fire tool set can be viewed as a basic primer in smithing. One might even choose an artist blacksmith for a larger architectural or sculptural project by inspecting her or his fireware craft. If the smith has successfully solved aesthetic and technical issues in a fire tool set, most other problems can be solved.

You may think a broom is a broom, but even these are varied and their shapes and colors important to a design. There are special companies that provide brooms in shapes and lengths ordered by the artists. Some may be added from commercial hardware store brooms and worked into the wrap around the tool shafts. Sometimes a brush is used rather than a broom. The way the broom is connected to the handle can be an art element, not simply a happenstance, or an expedient method. Note particularly the differences in size, shape, and color in the examples from Jerry A. Coe, Eric Clausen, Helmut Hillenkamp, and Gordon Kirby's brooms, to understand how they contribute to the overall look of the tool sets.

The casual viewer of ironwork, and especially of fire tool sets, is likely to miss the exciting aspects of working with the steel. They are particularly evident in fire tool sets that allow the artist to display his design abilities and his mastery of the medium. He can use detailing that might not be possible in the repetitive designs of a fence, or a staircase, for example.

A fireplace tool set is like a sculpture, completely three-dimensional but there's even greater latitude in design ideas because the stand is a separate item yet must be coordinated with the tools. There is the opportunity for the craftsman to use different joinery techniques that fascinate him. There are rivets, banding, twists, bends, and handles, tops and bottoms that can be manipulated and combined.

Daniel Miller's Wedge Fire Tool set, see page 109, has so many subtle nuances in its design that studying its assembly is a revealing exercise. Three curved pieces combine for the base and are banded together. The banding is repeated at the top to bundle the wedges that have upset endings to hold them in place. The handles of the shovel and poker have the same motif. These tools are pierced by the horizontal bar as the hanging device. Two tong handles are suspended at the back of the horizontal bar by two pegs protruding almost invisibly from the bar. The upright support, the shovel, and poker have a fascinating twist. The upset bar motif is repeated for the feet of the tripod.

Typical blacksmith joinery and techniques mentioned are all evident in the details of L. Japheth Howard's close-ups from a tool set made from flat tool stock. Similar detailing is evident in Stephen Bondi's more ornate tool set that is matched to a pair of andirons. Bondi's tools have traditional scrollwork that is reminiscent of Victorian, Rococo, and more ornamental styles than Howard's. All require the basic techniques and skills of the artist blacksmith.

L. Japheth Howard. Fireplace tools usually have a shovel, tongs, some kind of poker, and a brush or broom. They hang together on a stand that must be designed to support the weight of the tool, and be well balanced so it doesn't tip over when one or more of the tools are removed. *Photo, Jay Dotson*

111

Stephen Bondi. Often the fireplace tool set is matched, or coordinated, with the andirons and the screen or doors as in this ornate set composed of scrolls and twists. *Photo, artist* © Bondi Metals

For people who do not understand the iron forging processes used by blacksmiths, Stefan Dürst demonstrates how lengths of iron bars are turned into useful tools and objects. It boils down to the ability of metal to be shaped when it is hot. In this series Dürst illustrates a flat bar being heated in a forge, hammered, and drawn out to become a shovel, a poker, tongs, and other tools. Regardless of the result, the blacksmith deals with heating iron, and shaping it with hand and power tools. Tools may be finished with a patina, oils, and waxes to prevent rusting.

It's often hard for the layperson to understand how a tool set, or other ironwork objects evolve. Stefan Dürst shows how a piece of flat metal bar is forged to become a shovel, a poker, or another tool.

Begin with a flat bar for the tool handles.
Photo series, courtesy artist

The steel is heated in a forge, the metal is held with a tongs.

114

The hot metal bar end is spread out and flattened by hammering it on an anvil.

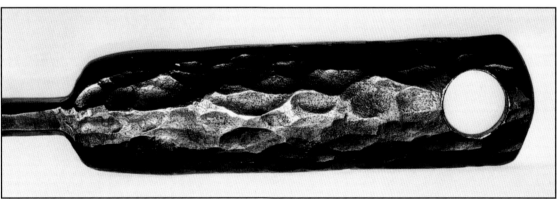

To finish, the handle is rounded slightly, textured, and a hole is made for hanging.

The opposite end is heated, drawn to a point, and then reheated as necessary…

…and bent to form the poker end

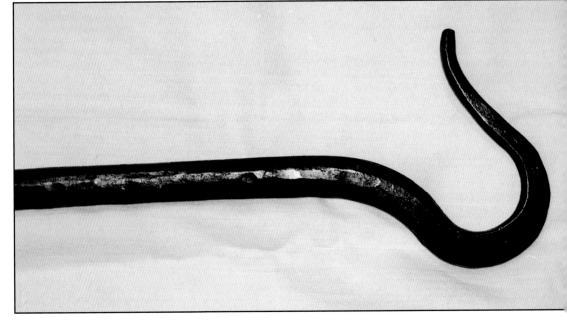

Another bar is made for the brush holder but the end must be split so it can be screwed to the brush mount.

The brush is mounted to the handle shaft with screws.

A third bar end is heated to become the shovel. It is drawn out, or flattened, under the power hammer.

The shovel and handle is all one piece made from the flat bar that is flattened, shaped, and textured.

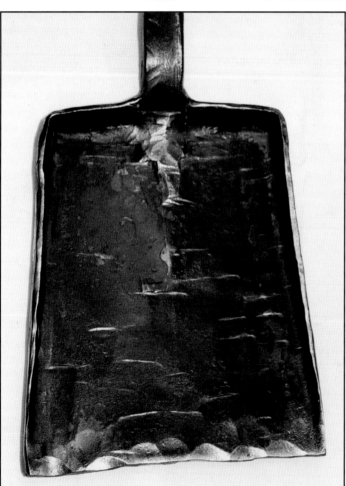

Stefan Dürst. A mounting rod is made from round bar. To screw it into the wall, a long screw end is welded on. A disc is welded on to hide the drilled hole in the wall. The three handles are suspended from the wall-mounted bracket. *Photo series, courtesy, Stefan Dürst.*

Jerry A. Coe brings his unique design concepts to fireplace tools made of forged bronze with a variety of finishes. Added details may be forged or they may be cast from clay into bronze. He often uses Art Nouveau styles as the take-off point for his tool sets that depart radically from traditional sets. Coe, who has traveled about the world extensively, also brings this multi-cultural viewpoint to his pieces. Additionally, his clients may be from many other countries so he has to consider their cultural backgrounds, as well.

Jerry A. Coe. Four tool sets and stands made for a castle in Genoa, Italy. The forged iron and bronze sets may use the traditional detailing of the ironworker, but Coe uses them in inventive relationships. Combining bronze with iron adds shine and glitter to the sculptural forms. *Photo, Richard Sargent*

Jerry A. Coe. Fire tools and stand using a scroll design. A coiled scroll is used for the tool handles, and the base uses a "fishtail" scroll. Forged bronze. *Photo, Richard Sargent*

Jerry A. Coe. Detail of above. *Photo, Richard Sargent*

Jerry A. Coe. Two fire tool sets. Forged bronze and copper. Design at left is Art Nouveau. At right, cattails. Forged brass and copper. *Photo, Richard Sargent*

Jerry A. Coe. Detail of cattails emphasizes the hanging devices for the tools and the spectacu-
lar texture. *Photo, Richard Sargent*

Jerry A. Coe. Big Bird fire tool set for the Willows and Mouse fire screen, see, page 62. Forged and cast bronze. *Photo, Richard Sargent*

Dan Nauman, a Wisconsin artist blacksmith, creates objects with clean lines and precise hammer strokes. His restoration pieces are always well researched for authenticity and the optimum use of materials and techniques. In the tool set with the S-shaped base, the client requested an Arts & Crafts look but still wanted a contemporary feeling. The result was this set so deftly executed that it appears to have been modeled by hand as though in clay, and resulted in a base that looks scalloped.

Dan Nauman. Arts & Crafts style fire tool stand with the feeling of clay modeling for the stand and tool shafts. 40" high. *Photo, George Lottermoser*

In contrast to the set with the scalloped base another set was to have a light and classic look for a home that had botanical motifs and murals. Nauman created leaves by the repoussé method using small stakes and hammers to shape them. The tool shafts were forged from a homemade die, then forge welded to round bars to complete the shafts.

Dan Nauman. Fire tools with a ruffle-like stand suggested flower edges for a client requesting a tool set with a botanical motif. The shovel is triangular. 36" high. *Photo, George Lottermoser*

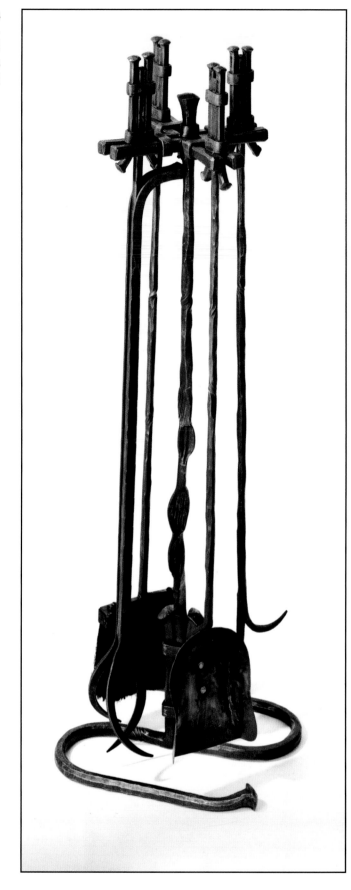

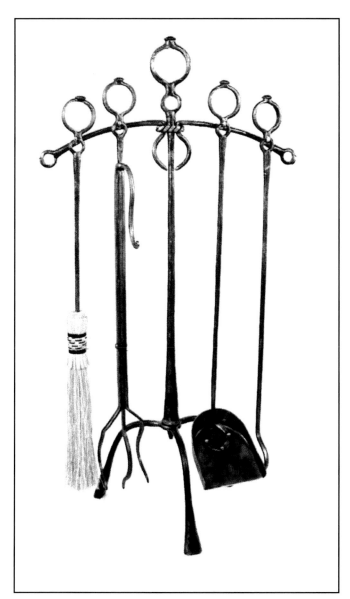

Tom Boone. Fire tool stand with a tripod base. Repeat circles in the tool handles and stand top, and the curved tool holder, are an attractive geometric treatment. *Photo, Donald H. Plummer*

Eric Clausen. Handles use a pineapple twist that makes the shaft appear as the skin of the fruit. The shovel edge is flared. The broom has rust colored bristles and the weaving around the top ties in with the shaft design. *Photo, artist*

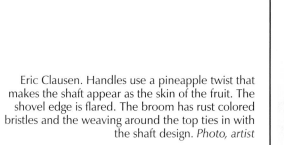

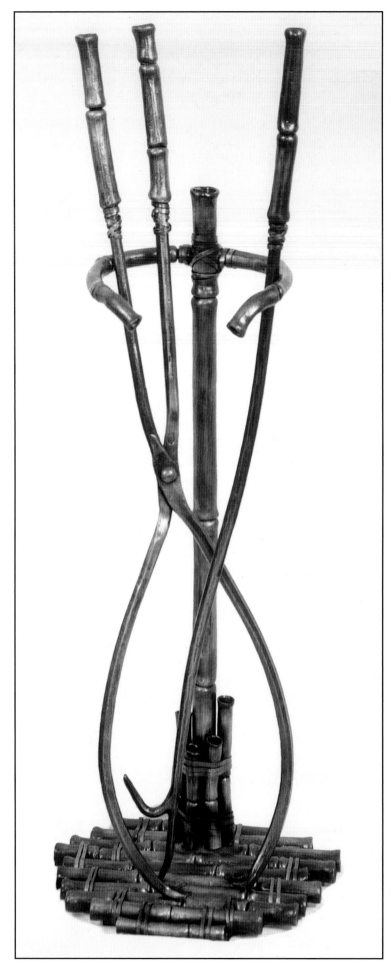

Helmut Hillenkamp. The challenge for creating this fire tool set was to overlay and combine triangles. The base is cut from an old piece of boilerplate. The broom bristles are in the same triangular shape as the metal pieces. *Photo, artist*

Joe Felber. Mild steel fireplace set with a bronze finish. The bamboo shaped fire tools on a banded bamboo looking base was made for a house decorated in an eastern style. *Photo, artist*

Opposite page: Frederic A. Crist and David W. Munn. A fire tool set with leaf handles and a floral shape. Observe the beautiful shape made by the negative space between the two leaf handles. *Photo, Frederic A. Cris*

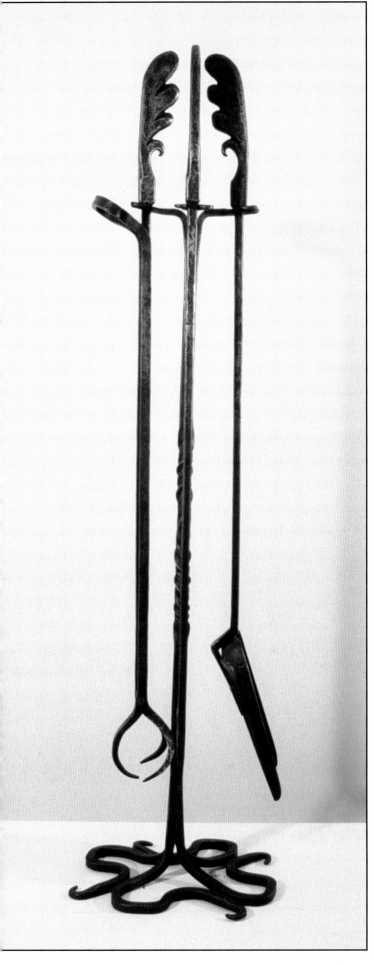

E. A. Chase, whose prodigious output has been an inspiration to this generation of smiths, creates fireplace related items using different combinations of metals. Now he uses mostly forged Chrome-moly steel (an alloy of 4140). This steel makes the tools stronger and lighter, and they can be made longer than is possible with more commonly used mild steel. He notes: "With today's large estate-sized fireplaces it makes servicing the fire more comfortable and people love them."

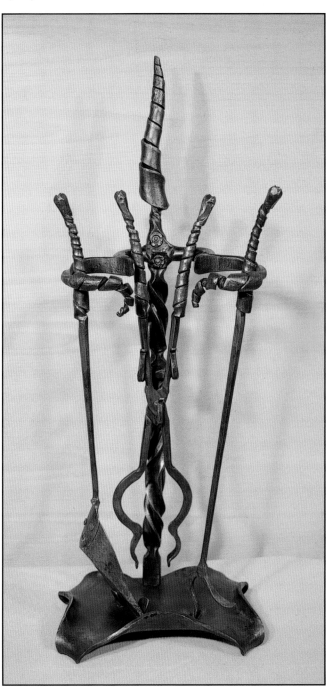

E. A. Chase. If one were thinking of personification in a fire tool set, this is what they might conjure. Twists, curves, coils, and a base that looks soft and clay-like give the set a Don Quixote-like appearance. Iron, chrome, steel, and brass. *Photo, artist*

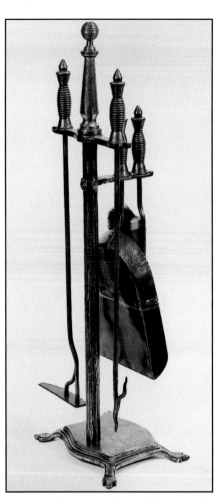

John H. Yust, architect-designer, with
Myron C. Hanson and Bill Krawczeski
Often, an architect for a project will
design the accessories for a fireplace so
they are in keeping with the total
appearance he wants to achieve. The
artist blacksmiths interpret and create
the design in metal. *Photo, Warren
Bruland*

Frederic A. Crist and David W. Munn.
Victorian fireplace tool set. The knob
tops were shaped into four sided pieces
instead of rounded, and a bronze ring
was added to the shaft handle. 40" high,
8" x 8" at base. *Photo, Frederic A. Crist*

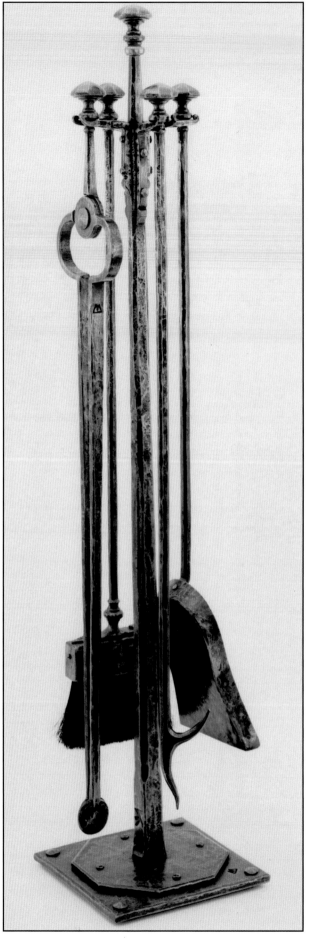

Often a project is a cooperative endeavor that taps the talents
of two or more people. Architect
John H. Yust designed the fire tool
set in steel with forged bronze
detailing for highlights. Two artist
blacksmiths, Myron C. Hanson
and Bill Krawczeski, created the
objects. Says Yust; "I wanted a tool
set with considerable weight in
the base and a low center of gravity so the stand would be stable.
There are no sharp edges on the
handles and they are easy to
grasp. The objective was to make
the tools well balanced and easily removable from the stand. The
wide dust pan and brush were
substituted for the traditionally
shaped broom and shovel."

Opposite page: Joseph Anderso
The angle of the tools is repeated
the angled base of the holder. Eac
tool handle is slightly different wi
an animal form on top. Bends in th
animal heads form the hooks f
holding them onto the bran
holder. *Photo, art*

Joseph Anderson. The central shaft is a branch with the tool holders as additional branches. The tool heads look like bats or mythical animal forms hanging from the branches. *Photo, artist*

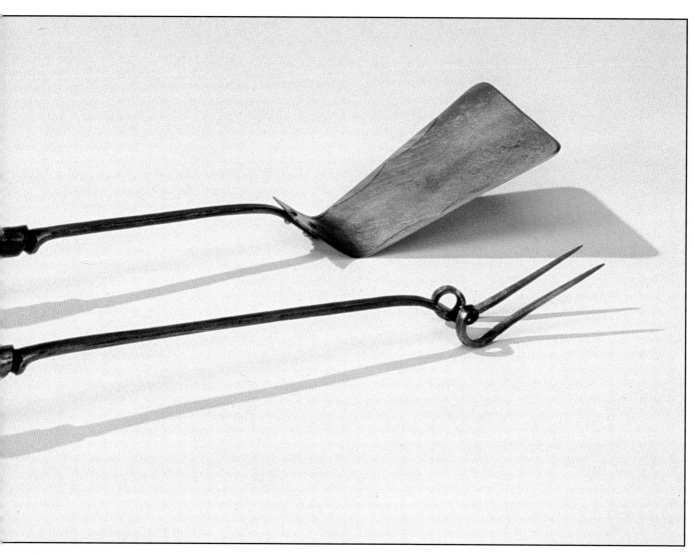

Joseph Anderson. Matching shovel and fork tined poker. The handle is riveted to the shovel in two places for stability and security. Constant variety in handle treatments and poker ends keeps the artist, and the viewer, amused and delighted. *Photo, artist*

There is infinite variety in the tools, handles, and detailing in pieces by Joseph Anderson. You have to smile when you look at them, be awed when you study the details, and assume the artist had as much fun making these animals, birds, twists, and turns, as you enjoy looking at them. His inventiveness of form within the confines of the tools' practicality makes them a welcome decorative item for those who buy them.

Joseph Anderson. Unique curves to the handles attest to the variety that can be created in basic tools. *Photo, artist*

Joseph Anderson. Pokers look like other world insects when laid out like this. Made with forged iron and bronze handles. *Photo, artist*

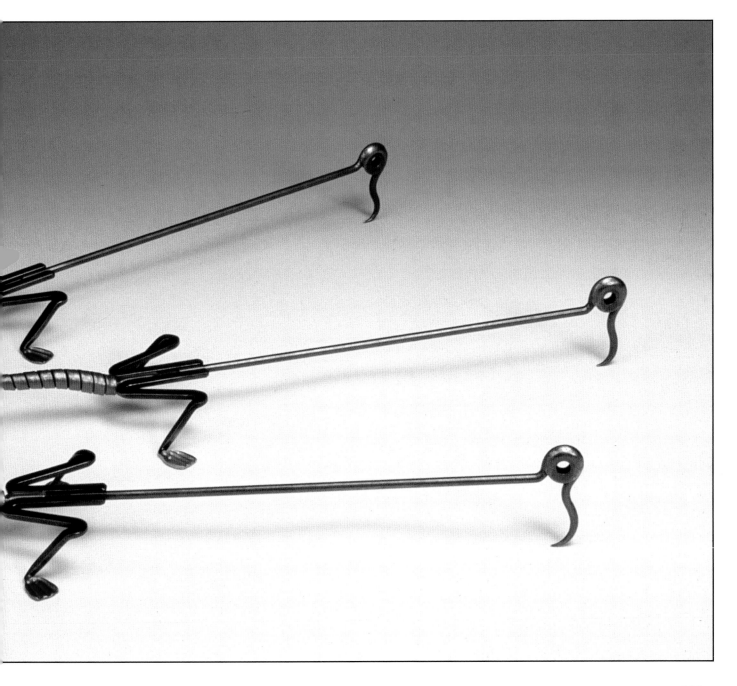

Michael Migala. The handles are made with the pineapple twist motif. All tool ends and the stand base are flattened by upsetting the steel. This means hammering the metal back into itself to create mass. The double lines near the handle tops were hot cut under a treadle hammer. *Photo, Jeff Bruce*

Gordon Kirby. Mild steel tool set with a design of repeated circles and a pineapple twist. *Photo, artist*

Jeff Fetty. Leaves "grow" up the center of the tripod fire tool stand and form a full cluster on top. The tool shanks are two sets of twists. *Photo, Gefeti*

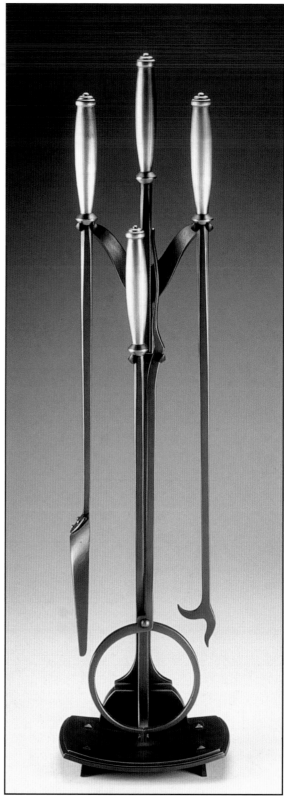

Occasionally, the cooperative endeavor in a workshop is among family members. In the Zanini workshop, in Cornuda, Italy, the father, Natalino, and his two sons work with him. Natalino had learned the blacksmithing art from his father, and he from his father. According to records, the house, or cottage, where the work was first done bears the date 1452 and has a declaration that this was "where a precious hammer first struck hot iron."

John Medwedeff. This set was designed for a New York interior decorator and has an architectural feel; clean, pristine, like a minimalist modern sculpture. *Photo, Jeff Bruce*

Natalino Zanini. Graduated sized twists in the handle and stand are characteristics of the Zanini workshop in Canuda, Italy. Additional twisted details are on the four feet of the unit. A bronze circular shape adds color and a contrasting smooth texture to the tactile surfaces of the tools. *Courtesy, artist*

In 1955 the Zanini workshop was awarded an honorary diploma for over three hundred years of continuous service, which means that it has been in the Zanini family since 1655. Today smiths in the workshop in Cornuda, a small town between the cities of Asolo and Venice, Italy, produce a variety of new and restoration works created with precise and scrupulous attention to details.

History and sailing ships were the inspiration for Michael Saari's fire tool set with triangles. He feels that sailing ship parts such as masts, spars, anchor flukes, and rigging forms, are great shapes dealing with structure, line, and fabricated and forged connections. They spell the nature of steel, involving line and structure, rather than solid mass. In his set the stand relates to a ship's vertical mast with a horizontal yard arm. Said Saari, "Here, as in a ship's construction, there is symmetry and balance. Utilizing old sailing ship forms in a new way with fireplace tools presents new thoughts about design and lightness. Assuring that the parts have balance and form along with aesthetic appearance is a challenging process."

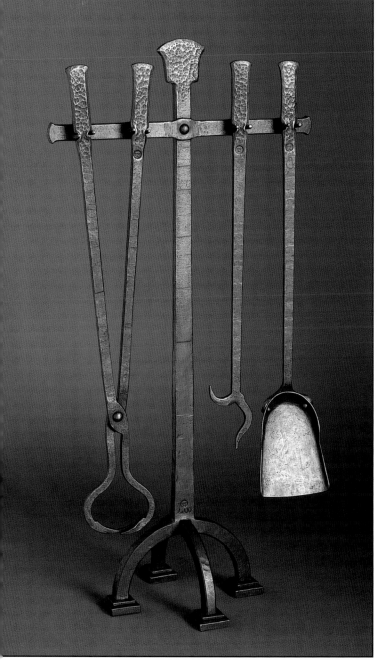

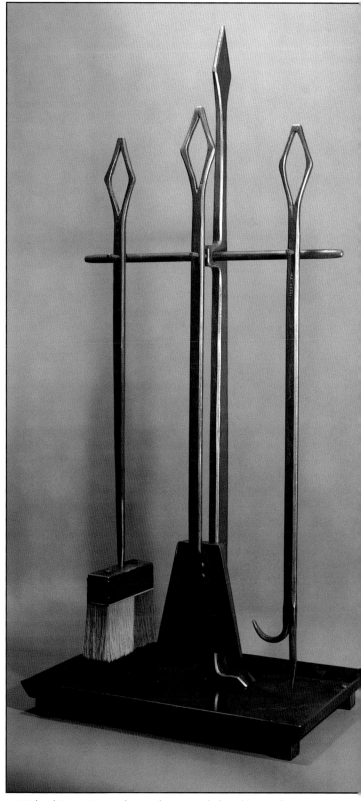

Michael Saari. A symphony of open and closed triangular shapes for the handles and the shovel make this tool sculptural and still very functional. Each tool hangs on a peg. The set is made of forged steel with a wire brushed and waxed finish. 36" high. *Courtesy, artist*

David Tuthill. Fire tools of forged steel made to match the fireplace surround, see page 187. The same use of flat bar stock and texturing tie the two together for a coordinated decorative, and expressive statement. *Photo, Jay Dotson*

139

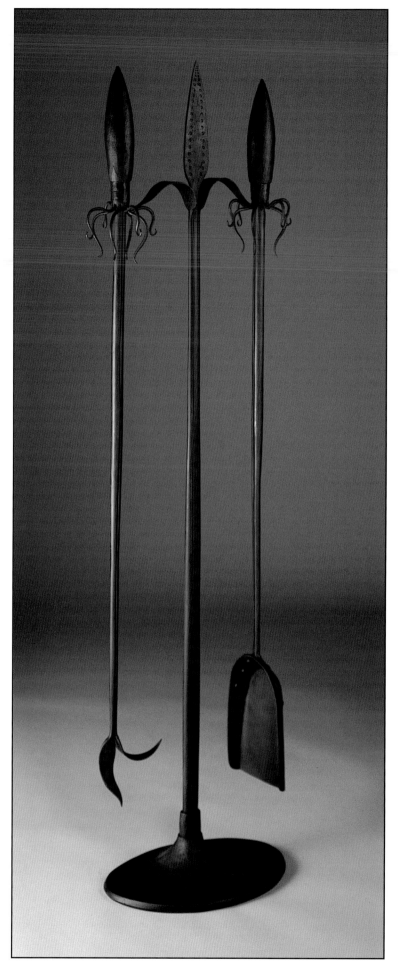

Eric Cuper. Squid fireplace set. The handles and their protrusions are a stylized form of a squid, a theme that appears in many of Cuper's forged pieces. *Courtesy, artist*

Frank Jackson. Organic shapes seem to grow as they would in nature in this fire tool set with grapevines and leaves. *Photo, artist*

Wall-hung Tools

All the tool sets shown so far have been free standing. Usually they are placed next to or near a wood-burning fireplace where they can be easily picked up to tend the fire. However, a tool set may also be hung on a wall bracket at the side or front of a fireplace. These present challenges to the creator. They are sculptural and three-dimensional but they are more likely to exist on a two-dimensional plane instead of in space, as does a three-dimensional set.

Paul Margetts achieves a sculptural balance by placing the shorter shovel and brush on either side of the longer poker and suspending all three from a horizontal bar. Each tool has a folded handle that fits over the bar and each can be removed and re-hung with no problem.

Paul Margetts. An Oriental inspired fire tool set has a matching fire basket, see page 175. *Photo, artist*

Maegan E. Crowley. Wall hung "Melting" fireplace tools hang as if they were slowly melting as a result of their function…heat. The hearth's stones inspired the hook shapes. Hanging the tools on the wall rather than clumping them together in a stand emphasizes their lines and shapes. 30" to 36" long. *Photo, artist*

Dan Nauman. Angled wall hung fire tools. Initially, when the artist and client thought of making the fire tools conform to the angle in the field stone wall, they laughed. Then they asked, "Why not?" and the result is this truly customized fire tool set with upset handle ends. 30" high. *Photo, artist*

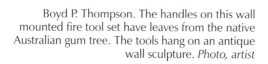

Boyd P. Thompson. The handles on this wall mounted fire tool set have leaves from the native Australian gum tree. The tools hang on an antique wall sculpture. *Photo, artist*

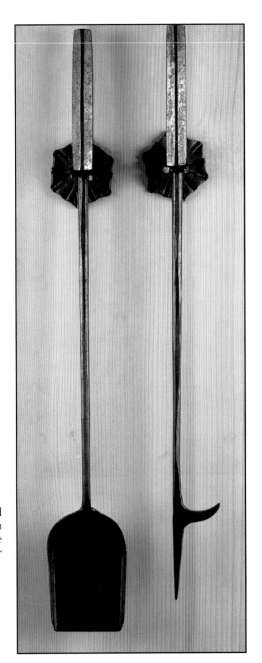

Joseph Anderson. Each of these whimsical looking tools hangs by a ring from a hook in the wall. *Courtesy, artist*

Russell Jaqua. Hexagonal shaped forged mild steel tools are mounted flat on the wall. Each has a pair of prongs that holds the tool to the rack. *Photo, Paul Boyer*

Mixed Materials

There's no rule stating that fire tool sets must be made entirely of steel. Steel has been used traditionally through the centuries and has proven more resistant to heat than other materials, which explains its practicality. Sometimes tools are more for display and décor than they are for use. When tools are not placed close to the fire, other materials can be introduced. Wood may be used for handles, as in Andrew Macdonalds' wall hung piece. Mixed metals are the choice of E. A. Chase. Dan Nauman combines steel with deer antlers, and Jerry Coe uses all stainless steel, or bronze, and even Lucite.

Andrew Macdonald reports that sometimes the design process is a surprise even to the artist. He wanted to use wood handles for a three-piece wall hanging set. When he finished designing it someone said, "Those look like gun handles." He was totally unaware of the similarities during the whole process. He was trying to make a form that felt good in the hands as well as counterbalancing the length. Guns were not part of Macdonald's life so he was surprised and mildly disappointed at the end result. He suggests receiving feedback during the design process that might eliminate such surprises.

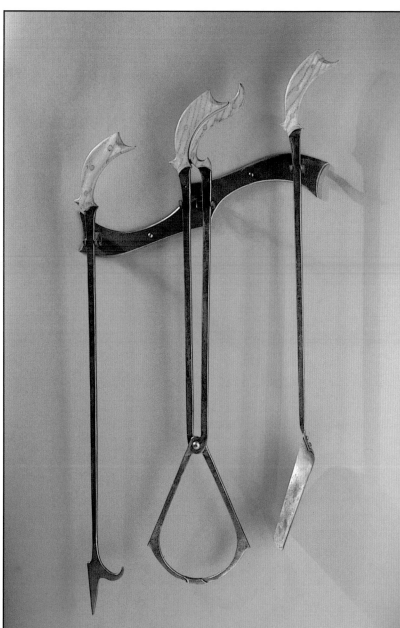

Andrew Macdonald. Wall hung mild steel fire tools with wooden handles.
Photo, Jeffery Bruce

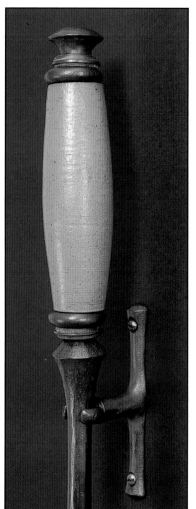

When Marc Mairona heard photos were needed for this book, he convinced his father to collaborate with him and create a piece that would be different. Different it is. It's the only example of a poker that has a stoneware handle. They had time for only this one piece, but several others are on their drawing board.

Thomas and Marc Maiorana. Forged iron poker with a thrown stoneware handle. This was a collaborative father and son project.
Photo, Marc Maiorana

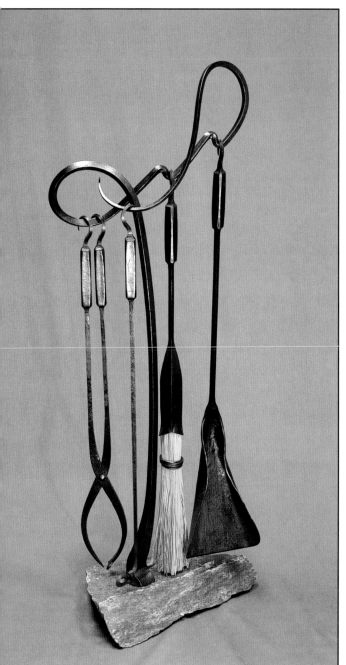

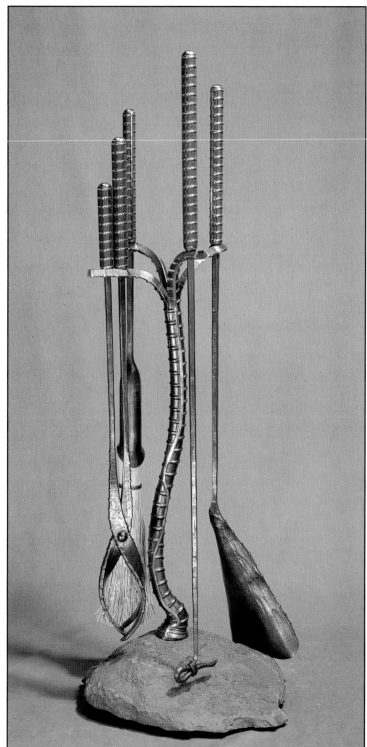

David Thompson. Tool set of mild steel on a stone base. 36" high. *Photo, Rebecca Ellis*

David Thompson. Forged reinforcing bar used for the shafts of tool handles. The base is stone. The poker end takes a fanciful turn. 34" high. *Photo, Rebecca Ellis*

Dan Nauman. Mild steel fire tools with a tripod stand and tool handles of deer antlers. Deer antlers grow in a consistent pattern but in erratic direction so the shafts carry out this feeling. *Photo, John Cumming*

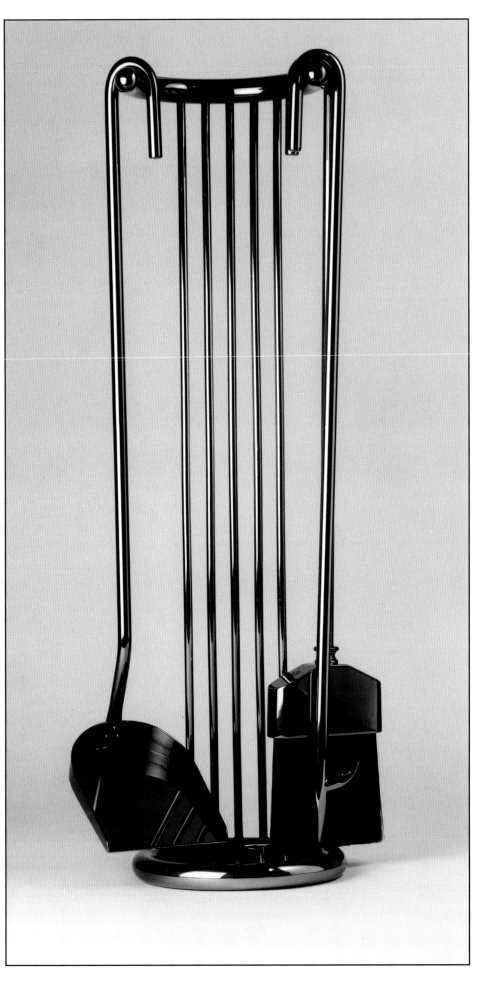

Jerry A. Coe. Forged bronze, chrome plated tools with a smoky patina in an Italian modern style. Made for a San Francisco, California residence. *Photo, Richard Sargent*

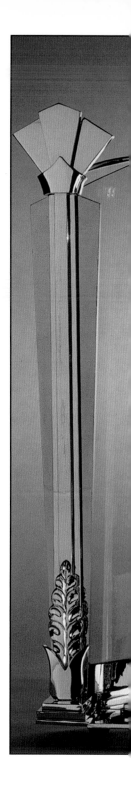

Jerry A. Coe. Fire tools and stand of forged bronze. French Provincial inspiration with oak leaves. For a residence in Napa Valley, California. *Photo, Richard Sargent*

Jerry A. Coe. Art Deco free standing fireplace screen. The screen frame is solid bronze, hand forged, silver plated, highly polished, and lacquered. Three separate pieces of glass are hand cut, hand beveled, carved, and slumped to create the necessary curvature. 36" high, 48" wide, 9" deep. *Photo, Richard Sargent*

Jerry A. Coe. Fire tools and stand for the Art Deco screen. Butterfly wings are cut from optical crystal. *Photo, Richard Sargent*

CHAPTER 5

Andirons, Grates, and Baskets

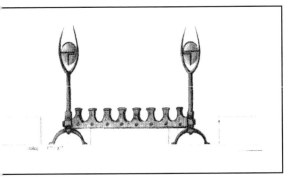

Douglas E. Wilson. Sketch for andirons with stones.

Andirons consist of a pair of metal supports for firewood used on a hearth. Each andiron is a decorative or plain vertical bar mounted on short legs with a horizontal bar behind it. They are made of heavy metal that can withstand the heat of a fire. A grate is a frame or a bed of iron bars used to hold the firewood and placed behind, between, or over the andirons. Grates, too, must be of very heavy iron because the heat of the fire could easily be as hot as the heat of a forge, and the metal could soften and belly over time, and with use.

Jerry A. Coe. Forked tongued animals become the andirons and their bodies are the grate's bars with their tails at the back. *Photo, Richard Sargent*

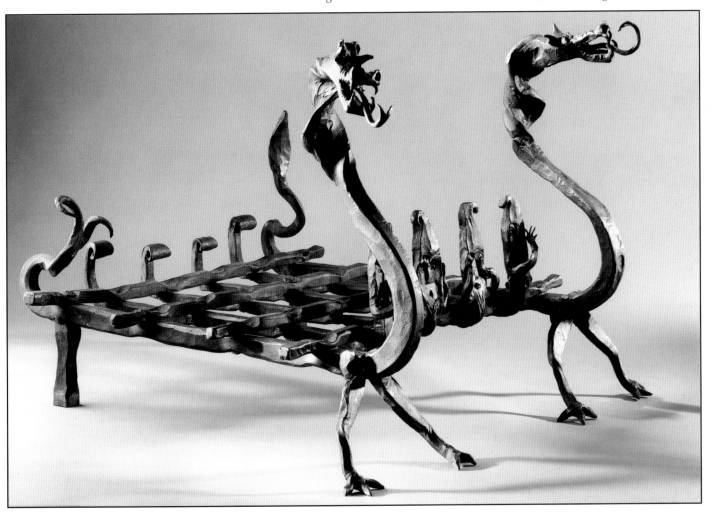

With the function of fireplaces changing over the years, andiron designs have changed, too. Before the invention of the gas stove, cooking was done in an open hearth. Fireplace accessories included tools and pots, and swinging steel arms hooks that held the pots, see Chapter 7.

Early fireplaces supplied heat to a room so they were quite large. The andirons were usually very tall; the grate was sturdy to hold heavy logs. The andirons for the Grove Park Inn in Asheville, North Carolina, are 6' high, and in scale with the 19' high opening of the huge fireplace built in 1913.

A common type of andiron of yore was tall with an open basket shape on top for keeping food and drinks warm. Hooks, called trammels, protruded from the vertical shaft so that a rod placed across the andirons on the hooks became a spit. A handle could be attached to the rod for turning it so that meat or a pig laced onto the rod could be roasted on all sides.

A pair of these andirons surfaced in a photo of a fireplace in the Jekyll Island Club Hotel on Jekyll Island, Georgia. It resembled the andirons made by Samuel Yellin, see Chapter 1. Knowing that Yellin's shop had created much of the ironwork for buildings along the eastern seaboard in the 1920s and 30s a search was begun for their maker, but there was no history of their origin. The Jekyll Island Club Hotel, dating from the early twenties, is one of the Historic Hotels of America. Public Relations director, Sue Anderson, interviewed several older members to get a feel of how the andirons were used. One man said they used to drink brandy in the Boar's Head Lobby, then put the bottles in the basket to let the brandy warm slowly to perfection while they retired to the pool parlor or card room.

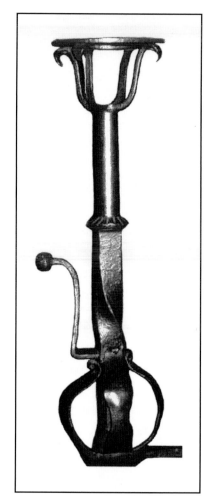

Jekyll Island Club Hotel. An andiron from about the 1920s showing the basket top and a handle for turning a spit on which meat was roasted. *Courtesy, Jekyll Island Club Hotel, Jekyll Island, Georgia*

Grove Park Inn. A pair of 6' high andirons is still used in the restored huge stone fireplace in the Grove Park Inn, Asheville, North Carolina. They date from the hotel's beginning in 1913. *Courtesy, Grove Park Inn, Asheville, North Carolina*

Often, such andirons were in a dining area as well as the kitchen. The Jekyll Island Club Hotel has 103 gas and wood burning fireplaces, each individually designed in the English Edwardian style that was high fashion at the time the hotel was built. The andirons throughout are like a history of the shapes used at the time. All the hotel fireplaces and their hardware exhibit beautiful detailing. Mantels are hand carved. Many have ceramic tile and marble surrounds, treatments with mirrors, Ionic and Tuscan columns, fleur-de-lis motifs in the woodwork, and other individualized, and intricate detailing.

Antique andirons continue to fascinate ironworkers, collectors, and people who want to restore a period style home or building. Many are exhibited in museums dedicated to early American furnishings. Keith Leavitt's client was restoring an elegant 1790s home on the east coast and wanted a pair of period andirons he had seen in Albert Sonn's book, "Early American Wrought Iron." As an alternative to traditional knobs or balls as finials, he asked for "whale-tail" volutes. He requested spit racks with a reversible warming tray explaining: "Perhaps our forefathers warmed soap stones but I plan to use my shelf for heating hot toddies."

Keith A. Leavitt. Whale Tail andirons for a 1790s restored house. The warming shelf replaces the spit rod and will be used for warming hot toddies. Leavitt's challenge was to build the andirons and log holder using only traditional joinery, such as rivets and tenons, as were used in the original andirons, and no modern welding techniques. 19" high, 18" wide, 18" deep. *Photo, Steven Dunn*

Bruno Corriani, of Lentiai, Italy, has built a reputation in Italy for both restoration and contemporary ironwork, for which he has earned several prizes. His andirons for a restored Italian building repeat the functional features of the Jekyll Island Club Hotel andirons. They are more decorative than the stark designs used in early America. Observe the use of the animal head on the bottom.

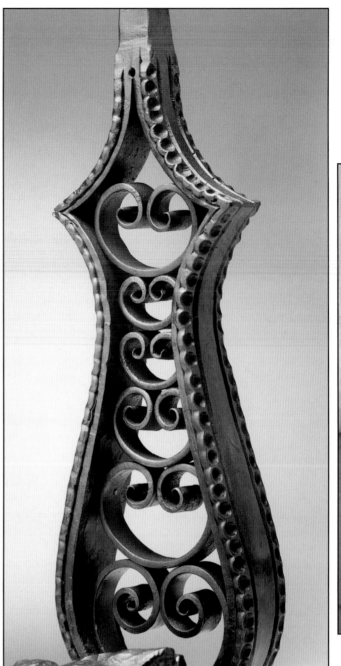

Bruno Corriani. Detail of the andiron shaft shows the scrollwork and ornamental edge. *Courtesy, artist*

Bruno Corriani. The same type of basket top can be found in andirons made for restoring period style fireplaces. Corriani's workshop in Lentiai, Italy, is often called upon to create and recreate historical Italianate styles. Here, the basket top is very ornate and lion heads appear at each end of the horizontal bar. *Courtesy, artist*

Carlo Rizzarda. Cat andirons. *Photo, Stephen Bondi*

Animals and animal heads on fireplace accessories have been used for years and in many countries. The pair of cats on a fender or guard by Carlo Rizzarda, (1883-1931), an Italian blacksmith, illustrates the clever use of animal forms. Rizzarda's work spanned the Art Nouveau and Art Deco periods.

There's nothing tentative about Jerry A. Coe's approach to hot metal. He is master of the medium and tackles it like a football player lunging at his opponent. He makes it bend, twist, and turn to his will. His andiron and grate combination, see page 152, is a two headed animal with other demons on the uprights between. One has his eyes covered; another has his hand to his face. Each animal head is different in the toss of its head, the lashing of its tongue, the twist of its neck and tail. He lets his imagination take over and his hands bend the iron to their bidding.

Joseph Anderson's fire dragons with tails are a figment of his imagination but he creates them with smiling, pleasant faces. Roland Greefkes "fire dog" andirons and grate are a subtle pun. They are, literally and figuratively, firedogs…. another name often used to describe andirons. Alan Drew places a frog atop each of the uprights on his andirons. Simon Benetton uses rams on one set and seahorses on another.

Joseph Anderson. These gentle looking animals seem to be talking to one another from their andiron perches. The andirons also sport the animals' tails. *Courtesy, artist*

Opposite page: Alan Drew. A different twist to the
ball motif on a set of andirons; a hand carved pair
of frogs rest on top. *Photo, Dorothy Stiegler*

Roland C. Greefkes. Firedog andirons The gnarly looking elements created with hot
metals and tools, have a softness, plasticity, and tactile quality. *Photo, artist*

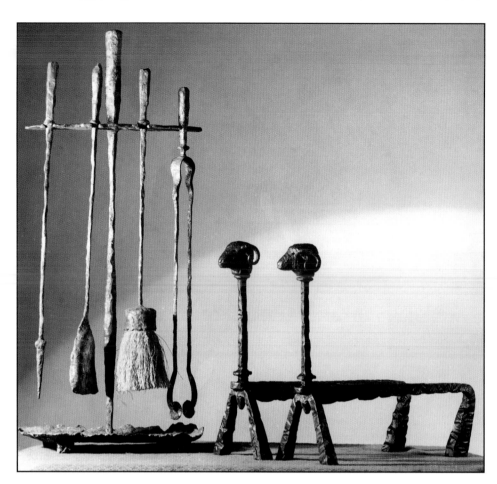

Simon Benetton. Lambs' heads andirons and tool set. *Courtesy artist*

Simon Benetton. Seahorse andirons and tool set. *Courtesy, artist*

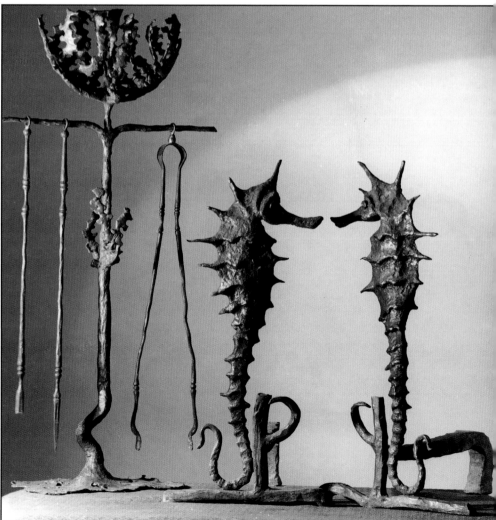

Nature's forms are also popular for andiron decoration and Lars Stanley's Lotus andirons are far right of traditional flower shapes or historical examples. Stanley's stint at the anvil with the hot iron illustrates how the lotus shape is raised from the four thick bars that support it. The iron ends are heated and flattened through many heats and much pounding until the metal is splayed and textured. The power hammer at the rear does much of the heavy flattening on the hot iron.

Lars Stanley. From forge to fireplace. Lars Stanley forges the Lotus andirons in his workshop. The lotus form has been taken from the fire using a pair of heavy duty tongs. It was shaped while hot in the power hammer at the rear. Fine detailing was created with hand tools. *Photo, Bill Kennedy*

Lars Stanley. The finished Lotus andirons front and side views. Four bars that form the stand were bundled together at the top of the shaft with forged collars. The central bars were split to form the top and bottom petals, and the side bars were used to form the side petals. *Photo, Atelier Wong*

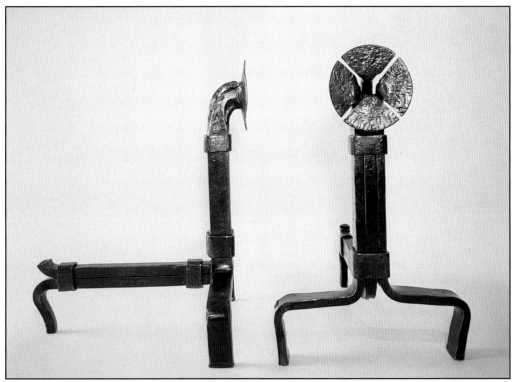

Lars Stanley. The Lotus andirons in situ in a contemporary fireplace setting. *Photo, Atelier Wong*

Douglas E. Wilson. Leaf andiron and grate of forge iron. Textured with hand hammering. Matchin poker. *Photo, Ken Woisar*

Douglas E. Wilson. Fire grate.
34" wide, 18" deep. *Photo,
Ken Woisard*

Craig Kaviar. Bronze andirons
with sunflowers and leaves.
Photo, artist

Within the context of these basic accessories, an amazing variety of designs and styles appear.

John Phillips has learned to design ironwork accessories in several styles. The pair of "basket" andirons has a series of traditional motifs such as scrolls, banding, and baskets. Baskets are made by twisting three or more hot iron bars as they are fastened at one end and twisted from the other end so the bars expand out and form the open look. The artist blacksmith brings many disciplines into each of his pieces; he has usually studied art and can see an object in three dimensions from his studies of sculpture. Phillips, like most other artist blacksmiths whose work is shown, has made railings, fences, furniture, and sculpture in addition to fireplace accessories.

John Phillips. Wheat twist andirons and log holder. *Photo, artist*

John Phillips. Basket design andirons. *Photo, artist*

Modern andirons are often simply shaped, and with interesting forms. Artists continually explore the nature of iron in new ways so that functional objects are fine art. David Tuthill's flat, notched and tapered andirons are made to match a steel surround for a remodeled gas fireplace. Lars Stanley takes one design cue from the flames of the fire itself. Jim Wallace's arrowhead shaped andirons, see page 165, have a bronze patina with bronze banding. They, too, are coordinated with the fire screen, see page 87. Daniel Miller's andirons, see page 165, are the personification of Clytemnestra, one of a pair of "characters" from a Greek tragedy of the Trojan War. On a facing fireplace, the personification of Agamemnon, the King, is ensconced.

David Tuthill. Andirons designed to coordinate with the surround for a remodeled fireplace (see page 80). *Photo, Jay Dotson*

Lars Stanley. The fire itself was the inspiration for these flame shaped andirons. The ends were tapered with the power hammer and bent while hot. *Photo, artist*

Lars Stanley. Tapered andirons with tops gently forged into facets. The 2-1/2" solid square uprights were punched and joined with mortise and tenon connections. *Photo, artist*

Lars Stanley. Pierced andirons. The uprights were forged from one single piece of solid steel and pierced while hot. *Photo, artist*

Jim Wallace. Forged mild steel andirons. 32" high. Collection, Mr. S. K. Johnston, Chattanooga, Tennessee. *Photo, Murray Riss*

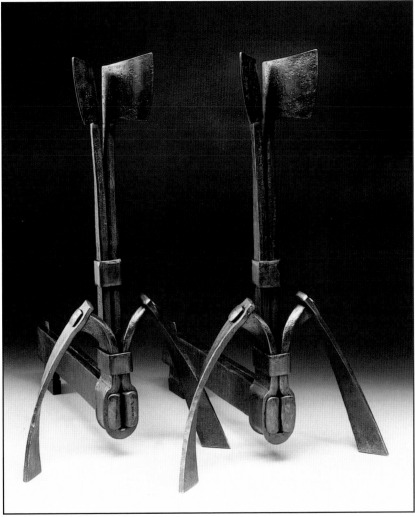

Daniel Miller. Clytemnestra Eyeing The King. The King is on a facing fireplace as though waiting for the play to proceed. *Photo, Weststar Photographic*

If they were in the same house as Daniel Miller's tragedy characters, and made by the same artist, one might think that Jefferson's Mack's andirons were a pair of soldiers waiting for the war to proceed. The fishtail scrolls at the tops resemble heads, the bent iron at the sides are arms, and the sturdy coils at the bottom appear as feet. Even if no symbolism were intended, one can always read imagery into an object.

Balls are a common motif for the tops of andiron shafts, but with some deft forging their shapes can be easily altered. The tops of Chris Axelsson's andirons began as balls, but they were upset and hammered into a half rounded shape made to jut forward rather than perch on top.

Chris Axelsson. A ball shape is upset to change its form. The shafts are chiseled in this museum reproduction. 29" high. *Photo, artist*

Jefferson Mack. Andirons appear to resemble soldiers guarding the fire. *Photo, Tom MacAffee*

167

The andirons with the bronze round balls by Lee Proctor take on a new aura when the balls are enclosed by a ring of iron, like the sun with a halo around it. A matching ball and ring top is on the fire tool set by Dan'l Moore, below. Keith Leavitt's andiron, see page 170, has graduated size twisted shafts, each topped with a ball forged into a pyramidal shape. The same detail is in the rivet heads at the bottom.

Seth Tyler. The rosettes and the curving shapes of these andirons were designed to accent similar shapes in the molding surrounding the fireplace. Forged brass, copper, and steel. 20" high, 18" deep. *Photo, George Lottermoser*

Lee Proctor and Dan'l Moore. Brass balls with iron "halos." Design and andirons by Lee Proctor. Matching fire tool set by Dan'l Moore. *Photo, Dan'l Moore*

Seth Tyler. A drawing of ducks evolved into this abstract pair of andirons made in stainless and mild steel. You can still the detect the ducks' winged feet in stainless steel. 20" high, 20" wide, 18" deep. *Photo, George Lottermoser*

In any one project, several disciplines and tools may be applied. When a client requested a fireplace grate representing Mount Katahdin, the most rugged mountain in Maine, Keith Leavitt had to call a variety of experiences and techniques into play. The client wanted to capture some of his passion for mountain climbing in his fireplace grate. The final grate is a painterly and sculptural composition of mild steel, stainless steel, and silicon bronze. Forged trunks were textured with a treadle hammer. A chisel, hand guided with a pair of tongs, was used to cut lines in the metal to simulate snow and fir trees. The foothill treetops were textured with a power hammer, and the pine tree silhouette was cut with a water jet.

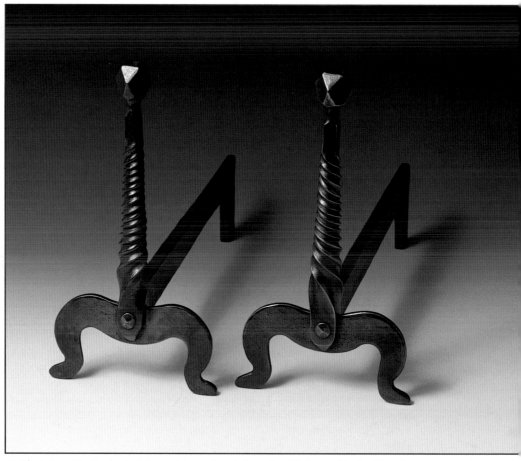

Keith A. Leavitt. Graduated size twists on the shaft ends with faceted balls. The client requested a traditional andiron "with a twist" and forward leaning balls. *Photo, Steven Dunn*

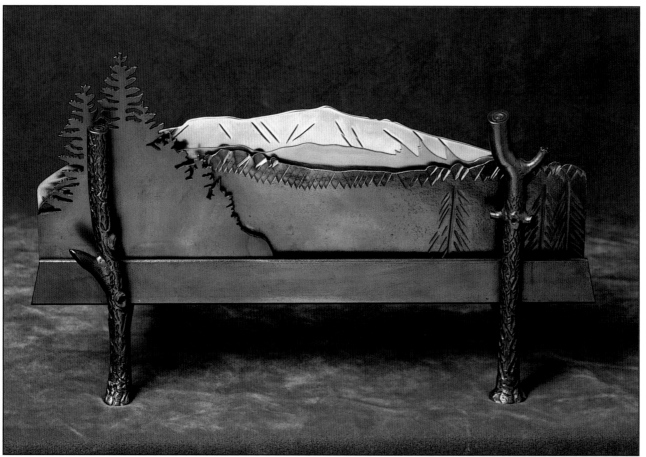

Keith A. Leavitt Mount Katahdin. fireplace grate Mild steel, stainless steel, and silicon bronze. Pine tree silhouette were cut with water jet. Hand chiseling was done on the snow and tree with power hammer texturing on the foothill treetops. *Photo Steven Dunn*

Log baskets give the artist blacksmith great leeway for imagination and virtuosity with the malleable metals. Natalino Zanini's animal head wood basket looks skeletal, like a two headed being with rings in the animal's noses. The rings serve as handles for moving the grate when necessary. The fire log basket's powerful looking elements with the upset ends make a strong statement for the use of iron in a functional and decorative manner. A pan below catches residue from the logs.

The various fire baskets shown range from medieval to modern in style. They may have been made to match or complement the fire tools and/or the fire doors. Sometimes they are made to stand alone as a decorative, functional sculptural item.

Russell Jaqua professes a genuine affection for making log baskets. He says, "Here is an application in which substantial material has great functionality. It is an excuse to create something elegant and beefy at the same time." His modern basket and andiron set is an example of freehand, open die stamping. Using the corner of open dies, he stamped the material to get alternating angular and curved lines. This complex pattern illustrates the aesthetic principle that an alternating line is a decorative line. (See page 177.)

Grove Park Inn. Huge logs were felled for the 19' fireplace at the Grove Park Inn and the best way to haul them from the forest to the fireplace was on a wheeled cart similar to those used in coal mines. This dates from 1913 and is still in use in the hotel. *Courtesy, Grove Park Inn, Asheville, North Carolina*

Natalo Zanini. Log Basket and grate. *Courtesy, artist*

Simon Benetton. Always an innovator, Benetton made the grate from a metal plate that he cut with a torch. *Courtesy, artist*

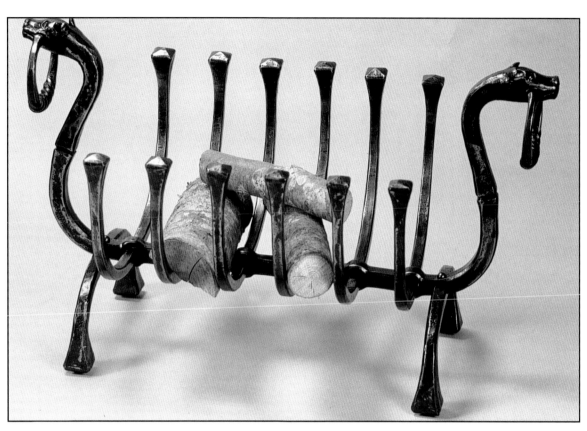

Natalo Zanini. Log Basket and grate with copper balls and a basket to catch ashes. *Courtesy, artist*

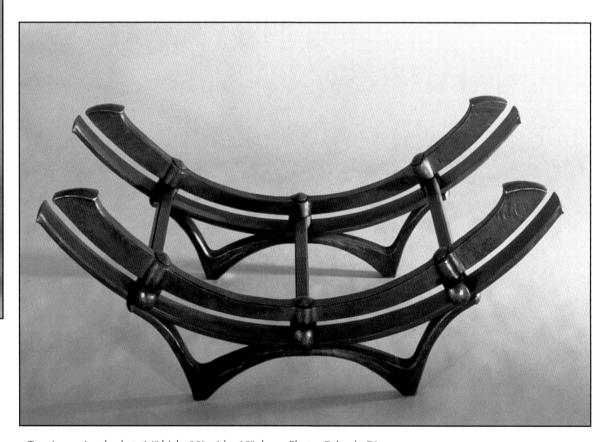

Tom Joyce. Log basket. 14" high, 38" wide, 18" deep. *Photo, Orlando Diaz*

Michael Bendele. Fire basket and grate made for a fireplace that is open on two sides.
16" high, 40" wide, 24" deep. The piece weighs about 300 lbs. *Photo, Jim King*

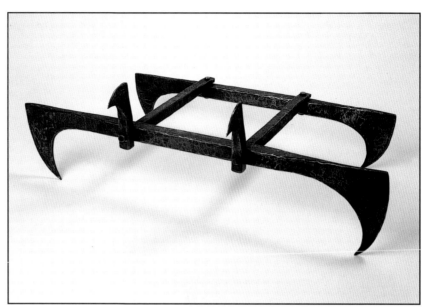

Steve Murdock. Fireplace grate has a coordinated log basket. *Photo, Phil Hoffmann*

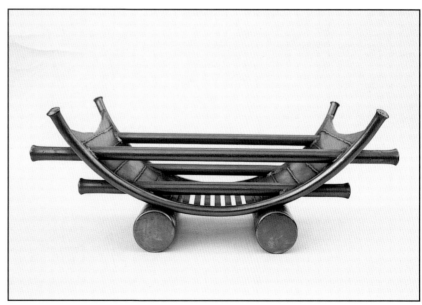

Paul Margetts. Oriental fire basket matches the tool set, see page 141. *Photo, artist*

Paul Margetts. Grapevine fire basket made for the coal man who supplies the coke for his forge. *Photo, artist*

Paul Margetts. Chinese puzzle fire log basket. Each element of the front, back, and sides is carefully woven together before welding in the style of a puzzle. *Photo, artist*

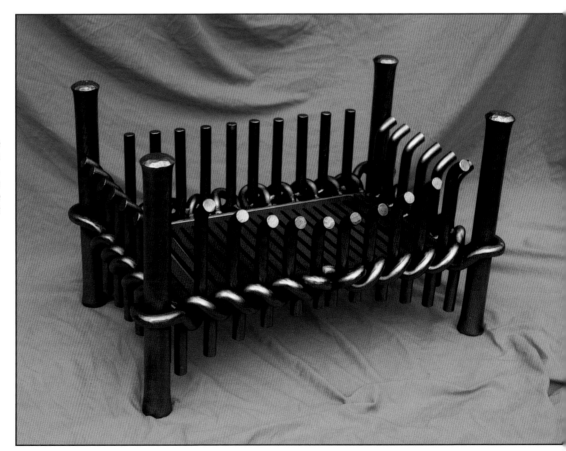

Russell Jaqua.
Rosette log basket
and andiron set.
Photo, Robert Gibeau

Paul Margetts. Chain fire log
basket. *Photo, artist*

177

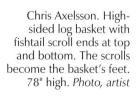

Russell Jaqua. Modern matching log basket and andiron set. The pattern is made with freehand held dies. *Photo, Robert Gibeau*

Chris Axelsson. High-sided log basket with fishtail scroll ends at top and bottom. The scrolls become the basket's feet. 78" high. *Photo, artist*

Greg Zwar. Rounded bottom fire log basket has a medieval appearance. *Photo, artist*

178

James Horrobin.
Fire log basket.
Photo, artist

Bob Bergman's fire basket is more functional than most because he has created a smaller basket above the main one for small scraps of wood. Sculpted faces on the top of the uprights represent old man winter. Carved heads top the handles of an accompanying fire tool set.

Bob Bergman. Fire basket with animal heads and matching fire tools. The basket has a smaller section for holding smaller pieces of wood. *Photo, artist*

CHAPTER 6

Surrounds, Stoves, and Ovens

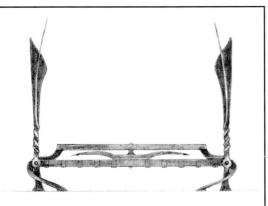

Douglas E. Wilson. Drawing for an andiron.

Throughout the book, accessories for interiors have included doors, tools, grates, and andirons, but there are more. There are surrounds, hoods, stoves, safety fire doors, and outdoor fireplaces. The following are only a sample of what's available in new items and ideas, and restoration projects. A fireplace "surround" is, as the name implies, the decorative element that surrounds the hearth opening. It is sometimes called the "facing," and does not include the stonework or brickwork of which the entire fireplace is composed. The surround is often coordinated, design-wise, with the fireplace doors and other hardware. It doesn't include the mantel, for example, though some surrounds incorporate the mantel as well. Surrounds may be made of the same materials as the fireplace doors, or a complementary material. Often a surround is used to update an existing fireplace. Simon Benetton's elaborate multi-level surround is composed of three panels. The central panel of copper has been cut with a laser beam. The side panels, made of wrought iron and colored glass, have lighting behind them for a dramatic effect. Matching fireplace doors and a coordinated fire tool set add up to a dramatic fireplace that is the focal point for the room.

Simon Benetton. Fireplace surround made in multiple layers. The central panel is copper that has been cut by a laser beam. The iron side panels have colored glass additions with lighting behind them. An iron and crystal fire screen has matching iron accessories with glass and copper trim. *Courtesy, artist*

E. A. Lee. A copper fireplace surround is 8' high, 5' wide. Matching andirons have octahedral heads and the fire tools have pineapple twist handles. *Photo, Eric Figg*

E. A. Chase. A brass and copper fireplace surround is
richly detailed with flora and fauna. A matching panel is
made to span the area below the mantel. *Photo, artist*

Craig Kaviar. Before. This shows how a surround can be an ideal solution for changing and/or updating an existing fireplace. The client felt the original tile fireplace was outdated. *Photo, artist*

Craig Kaviar. After. The addition of a copper surround with rich detailing, and a custom made fireplace tool set, completely altered the look of the fireplace in a remodeled house. *Photo, artist*

Craig Kaviar. Detail of the leaves and pattern around the edge of the surround. *Photo, artist*

David Tuthill's fireplace surround for a remodeled house is one of two that he designed and created for upstairs and downstairs gas burning fireplaces, each quite different. The unit is made of mosaic tile from Italy that was installed onto the facing after the metal work was completed. Steel and bronze elements were forged and fabricated. Fire tools were not needed as this is a gas-burning fireplace.

David Tuthill. Forged steel and bronze surround and a removable screen. Coordinated lights above the fireplace are forged and fabricated steel with mica. *Photo, artist*

John Phillips. A steel fireplace surround is carefully brush finished to create a subtle surface design and texture. Created for the Southern Accents Show House, 2001. *Photo, Mark Vaughn*

Dorothy Stiegler. Surround and screen are incorporated into one unit for a red brick fireplace. The metal has been patinaed to complement the red brick. *Photo, Cary Lowney*

In remodeling a restaurant in Atlanta, Georgia, Architect Ed Seiber's designers created a free standing wood-clad fireplace facing the restaurant's main entrance. It has a custom made metal screen that conceals a semi-private dining area beyond. The open square above the fireplace lets diners see through to the other part of the restaurant. The first illustration shows the view from the restaurant entrance. The second illustration shows the same fireplace from the private dining room side. It makes economic sense, and is a clever solution for dividing space efficiently, attractively, and functionally.

Seiber Design, Inc. Restaurants have more space latitude than private homes for innovative and dramatic fireplace treatments. A fireplace works as camouflage at Garrison's at Medlock Crossing Restaurant in Atlanta, Georgia. A free-standing wood-clad fireplace opposite the main entrance has a custom made metal screen that conceals the semi-private dining area beyond. *Photo, Thomas Watkins*

Seiber Design, Inc. The dining room area has the same fireplace detailing but it appears very different in the more formal surroundings.
Photo, Thomas Watkin

Another unique solution for a problem area is Scott Behr's curving and matching doors for a fireplace and a television set. In this remodeled New York apartment, an S-curve wall housed each unit in one of its curves. One set of doors had to curve outward, the other pull inward; not an easy task to complete, given the materials used. Closed and open views are shown.

Scott Behr. Matching fireplace doors and television cabinet custom made for an S-curve wall. Closed view. *Photo, artist*

Scott Behr. Open view of the S-curve wall solution. Each fireplace door opens on a pivot to accommodate the curve. *Photo, artist*

Alternate Fireplace Options

Our forefathers used their fireplaces for cooking before the advent of modern stoves. Still, some people enjoy the idea of authentic style hardware in their homes and the artist blacksmith remains the power behind the remodel. Even stoves sold commercially, rather than customized, owe their birth to the hand of the master metal worker.

Stoves by several manufacturers can be found in fireplace stores. A search for STOVES on the Internet will bring up a variety of sources and resources. Rais and Wittus, Inc., market a line of round steel stoves with glass doors. The steel doors slide back for viewing as an open hearth or, when closed, the unit can be used as a stove. A grill rack is also available.

Rais & Wittus, Inc. The "Rais 4" is a commercially marketed round stove available with steel or modern glass doors. The steel doors slide back for viewing the fire, or for heat. When closed the unit can be used for cooking. Other models are available. *Courtesy, Rais & Wittus, Inc.*

The ambitious fireplace with customized accessories by Michael and Stephen Bondi tested their ingenuity. They passed with flying colors and the help of a Nazel B-2 forging hammer for the power needed to achieve a very "plastic" feeling in the steel. Stephen Bondi explains that the people who commissioned this central room round fireplace for their private residence in Carmel, California, wanted a place where they could sit around the fire pot and look out through a large picture window over the Carmel/Pt. Lobos/Big Sur coastline.

Stephen and
Michael Bondi
© Bondi
Metals.
Custom
designed
fireplace with
grillwork over
steel. The
sheet metal
hood and
stack are
encased in
decorative
steel bars
hammered to
give the unit a
soft plastic
look. *Photo,
Stephen Bondi*

191

A close-up of the base unit. The firepot is half of an old buoy they bought from a shipyard. Edges were worked as with the hood's grillwork but much more intensively. The base has the same "vocabulary" of abstract shapes as the grillwork, only smaller in scale and more extensive. The rim has a ceramic tile ledge so that people can sit around the fire pot. One space in the tile area is left open; it has the fire tools hanging like billiard cues in a rack. The space allows someone to move in close and tend the fire.

Stephen and Michael Bondi. ©Bondi Metals. Fire pot made from half of an old buoy. The base has the same vocabulary of abstract shapes as the hood grillwork only on a smaller scale and more extensive. Ceramic tile ledge allows people to sit around the fire. Fireplace tools hang in the open area where one can get closer to the fire to tend it. *Photo, Stephen Bondi*

The hood and stack assembly was made to order by a sheet metal shop. The Bondi's then created grillwork to go around the hood. These vertical and horizontal bars were worked by heating and upsetting the edges back on themselves to achieve a soft character. The second photo shows the decorative grillwork close-up. The idea was to give the grillwork a soft character to contrast with the starkness of the sheet metal hood assembly. It was then that the Nazel Hammer was put to work on the grillwork to result in the softened sculptural effect.

Stephen and Michael Bondi. ©Bondi Metals. Detail of the grillwork on the stack and hood after working the bars with a power hammer to change their character. *Photo, Stephen Bondi*

Restorations are always a challenge for those who work on them. Bill and Tracey Veillette, of Amherst, New Hampshire, bought the 18th Century home of Colonel Robert Means, a house listed on the National Register of Historic Places, and the subject of "The White Pine Series of Architectural Monographs." They discovered that the original 18th Century cooking fireplace had been cut out of the floor and lowered into the crawl space below where it had been abandoned. A new ceramic tile floor had been installed over it in the kitchen. The original cooking fireplace, 18th Century brick, fireplace crane, and bake oven door were gone. Only a chimney with a flue for a wood burning stove remained.

"Our goal," said Veillette, "was to reconstruct the cooking fireplace and bake oven based on available research and evidence. The existing hearth gave us a clue as to the scale and massing. We retrieved enough 18th Century brick from the front sidewalk. Salvaged board for paneling came from an attic floor in Vermont and from Tony Hall, the joiner. All that was missing was the ironwork stove, doors, and fireplace hardware."

The Veillette's commissioned artist blacksmith David Court to make a bake oven door, ash pit door, fireplace crane, and lintel with attached arms that served as glove warmers.

Graham Pendlebury, the mason, had an antique cast iron bake oven door with an integral damper that Court used as a template for the dimensions and construction of the wrought iron door unit. The ash pit door was sized slightly smaller than the bake oven door that was typical of the period. The crane is a reproduction of one that appears in a reference book.

There were two minor changes. The first was that the integral damper to the bake oven door was more typical of the 19th Century before the introduction of cast iron cooking stoves. Second, the adjustable feature of the crane was more common in England and rarely seen in the colonies, except in Pennsylvania, where several have been documented.

To everyone's delight, the fireplace and bake oven are fully functioning.

The bake oven door under construction. The arched portion of the door unit will support the bake oven's brick dome. The ash door is in place below. Masonry is by Graham Pendlebury using 18th Century salvaged brick taken from the front pathway. White lime mortar. *Photo, Andrew M. Virzi*

David A. Court. Reconstruction of an 18th Century bake oven and door with a damper. A weighted vent cover in the center can be opened and closed for cooling the oven. Home and project of Bill and Tracy Veillette. *Photo, Andrew M. Virzi*

David A. Court. The final installation with andirons and cooking pot. The fully functional fireplace is used for cooking and baking. *Photo, Bill Veillette*

David A. Court. A fireplace crane made with dovetails, and mortise and tenon joinery. The center arm adjusts to raise or lower pots suspended from the hooks without having to remove them from the crane. *Photo, Bill Veillette*

The top of the fireplace oven is enclosed in a dome made of three layers of rolled brick and coated with plaster for additional fire protection. *Photo, Andrew M. Virzi*

Dan Nauman. A fireplace crane slightly modified from the historical interpretation from a straight arm to a curved arm for practical construction requirements. The arm swings to accommodate the hanging pots. *Photo, George Lottermoser*

Craig Kaviar. Outdoor fireplace doors for a farm incinerator. *Photo, Steven Drake*

Dan Nauman's fireplace crane and lintel with pots show how the blacksmith can recreate period items though sometimes slight changes are required depending on the situation. The design for this fireplace crane was derived from an existing piece in Pennsylvania, sketched in Albert Sonn's book, "Early American Wrought Iron." The problem was that the client wanted the top horizontal arm to be a specific height off the ground but the builder had already installed the pintle, which is the upright bar and pins on which the arm had to turn. Nauman had to modify the design by making the arm sweep up from the vertical shaft to rise above the pintle.

197

Russell Jaqua. Fire doors for the Port Townsend City Library, Port Townsend, Washington, were designed to contain fire for security reasons rather than to reveal or use fire. Closed position. *Photo, Robert Gibeau*

Russell Jaqua. Fire doors, open. To contrast with the plain fabrication of steel plate, traditional forging techniques were used for every functional detail. Hinges, bolts, and rivet construction illustrate the decorative possibilities forging techniques can bring to a project. *Photo, Robert Gibeau*

C. Carl Jennings. Hand built stove with decorative and functional surround.
Vents are used for air intake. *Photo, Hugo Steccati*

The blue, steam-spewing, roaring, dragon stove by Peter A. Krush is a feat of imagination, engineering, and pure fun. The functional stove, constructed of forged and fabricated mild steel, is built around a commercial firebrick lined wood stove. Mouth and nostrils are copper with stainless steel teeth. A water tank is hidden in the dragon's tail. A key is inserted into a hole in the tail and when turned a small amount of water is released through a ball valve. When the water reaches the hot chamber via a tube it flashes to steam. The steam travels out another pipe and through a calliope tube hidden in the neck, causing the dragon to "roar." The spent steam then escapes through the dragon's nostrils.

Fire in the firebox is viewed through a round glass door in the dragon's chest. Light from the firebox is also transmitted to the eyes via fiber optic cables. The dragon weighs approximately 450 lbs. Casters under the feet, and a removable head, tail, and wings, facilitate moving the dragon.

Peter A. Krusch. Stoves can take many forms given the patience and ability of a metal worker to create his vision. This functional wood burning stove is constructed around a commercial firebrick lined stove. Forged and fabricated mild steel, and copper with stainless steel teeth. 7.4' high, 4.5' wide, 4.2' deep. *Photo, Mark Council*

Simon Benetton. Maquette for a large
outdoor fireplace using iron sheet
metal with colored glass blocks.
Courtesy, artist

Simon Benetton. Maquette for a large circular fireplace made with
shaped sheet metal and cast elements. *Courtesy, artist*

Simon Benetton. Wrought iron fireplace with cast iron decorative elements. *Courtesy, artist*

Simon Benetton. Wrought iron fireplace with hood and etched details. *Courtesy, artist*

Copper hoods are as modern today as they were fifty to sixty years ago. Chris Axelsson's client liked the old hood over her fireplace but wanted to camouflage a dated, not so aesthetic, but still efficient, wood burning stove beneath. Axelsson made a copper surround to fit below the existing hood that covered the stove, and updated the look for the fireplace.

Chris Axelsson. A surround and screen made to fit beneath an existing copper fireplace hood from the 1920s. *Photo, artist*

Chris Axelsson. An existing hood from the 1920s that will remain but the wood burning stove will be replaced and the new surround will fit beneath the hood for a contemporary look. *Photo, artist*

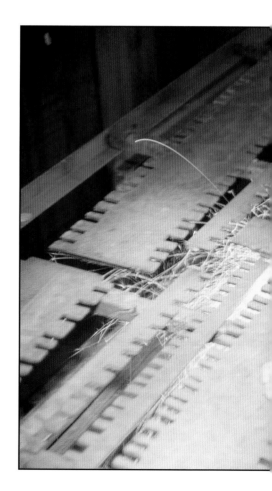

204

Jan Sanchez's client wanted a copper hood that would be in keeping with her Frank Lloyd Wright style home. Sanchez created a copper hood with textured panels inspired by textures in Wright's "Hollyhock House" in Los Angeles, California. The room was paneled in a dark mahogany wood, with custom bricks flanking the mouth of the fireplace. The floor was finished with large dark slate slabs that create a strong organic feel with windows that look out over the Pacific Ocean. Floor to ceiling windows and large sliding wood doors open out onto the hillside and a fountain that creates a view inspired by Frank Lloyd Wright's building, "Falling Waters."

Jan Sanchez. An in-process series shows several steps involved in making a copper fireplace hood. Here is the hood after installation with the work tags still hanging. The room décor will be dark mahogany wood paneling with custom bricks flanking the fireplace opening. *Courtesy, artist*

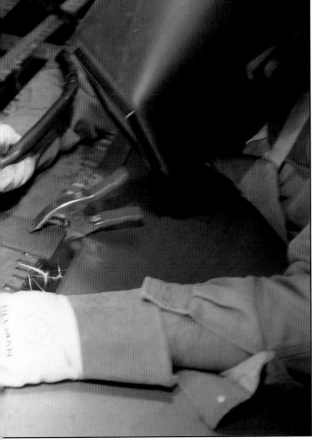

Jan Sanchez. To make the hood, patterns are placed on the copper, and the artist uses a plasma cutting torch. Plasma units can cut through materials quickly leaving only a minor amount of slag to clean away. *Courtesy, artist*

Jan Sanchez. Interior structural supports and straps must be installed. Two gauges of copper are used for extra strength and support. *Courtesy, artist*

Jan Sanchez. The finished 3 panels positioned and ready for installation. The embossed surface with a green patina design was inspired by a style used in Frank Lloyd Wright's "Hollyhock House." *Courtesy, artist*

C. Carl Jennings. Copper hood decorates an otherwise plain brick fireplace. *Photo, Hugo Steccati*

A silver teapot in the form of a hot oven mitt may be the ultimate and most unique fireplace accessory. Silversmith and metalworker, Jennifer L. Monroe, was making a similar mitt from iron but was still working on it at deadline time. The thumb is the spout, and at the top is a flip down lid, shown here in the up, or open, position. Said Monroe; "I like to explore concepts and perceptions through my choice of form. My work is functional but it challenges positions given to material items. By using a bold iconographic vocabulary, my work questions the viewer's beliefs and values." She also enjoys exploring the forms of metal and different surface enhancements possible.

One more possibility has been pictured in advertisements for home decorating accessories. Place candle holders with 5 or 6 arms for holding candles at different heights in the fireplace for evenings when you want the fire's effect but you don't want to light a fire. The candles will give off a glow and an aroma if you select scented candles. Wrought iron candle holders are particularly suitable to a fireplace, but any assortment of candle holders and candles will work.

Jennifer L. Monroe. "May I Serve You" may be the ultimate artistic fireplace accessory; a silver sculptural teapot that looks like a hot oven mitt complete with padding and pattern.

Glenn F. Gilmore. Free standing screen within a frame with matching tools. The surround, screen, tools, and stand are made with naval bronze. The frame was forged and patterned with dies made by the artist. Vertical and horizontal bars have fluted edges that repeat the fluted woodwork in the room. All bronze has a light chocolate brown patina applied and waxed. *Photo, McNabb Studio*

Glenn F. Gilmore. A portion of the steering wheel on a nautical theme fireplace screen. Color, texture, unique design elements are evident.
Photo, John McNabb

Chapter 7

A Gallery of Details

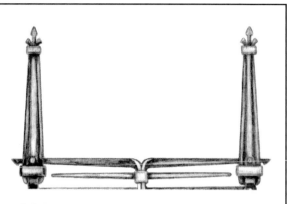

Douglas E. Wilson. Drawing for Fleur-de-lis andirons.

Focusing on details of fireplace accessories is a treat for the eye and mind. Often, the details on doors, tools, and andirons raise them from the ordinary to extraordinary. Throughout the book, several details have been shown, but this chapter presents additional close-up photos of edges, joinery, handles, hinges, and supports that can be easily missed in photos of entire pieces. Textures, patterns, colors, subtle carvings, and animal forms that grace many of the objects illustrated are often works of art in themselves. Details may raise your awareness of what can be done when you are contemplating fireplace accessories. They will provide unending ideas for the client and the custom ironworker responsible for developing unique designs.

"Ships Wheel" fire screen by Glenn F. Gilmore has rich colors, varied details, and a unique composition. Realistic forged iron ropes hanging at the top, coils on the handles, bronze center plates, a bronze center panel and rivets, all contribute to the color and artistry of the piece.

Details from Gilmore's Rose Blossom Screen show how the steel frame and copper blossoms are major color elements. The roses were treated with a torch so the flame would oxidize the metal and produce additional color nuances. Stainless steel wire mesh screen is another color and texture contrast to the mild steel branches and copper blossoms.

Glenn F. Gilmore. Detail of Rose Fire Screen, see page 8. Five different patterns were required to create the rows of petals in the roses. Oxidizing the metal with a torch yielded different colors. A clear overcoat was sprayed on. Observe the hand forged handle and how perfectly the frame was formed to fit around the marble columns. *Photo, John McNabb*

Textures, in addition to colors, are crucial to the artistic potential of metal. The artist knows he can enhance colors of the surrounding stone, brick or tile, provide visual interest, and a change in the reflections of light from the flames, and from exterior lighting.

Eric Clausen. Close-up of pomegranates, leaves, and branches illustrate the detailing that can be achieved in ironwork. *Photo, artist*

Frederic A. Crist and David W. Munn. Summer fire screen detail. C-scrolls, banding, and birds. Collection, Mike and Mary Lou Degrassie. *Photo, artist*

Michael Bondi's Japanese influenced screen with bonsai trees uses repoussé copper panels for texture and pattern. The raised surfaces resulted in subtle color differentiation within the same metal. Bronze screening introduced another color. Bruce W. Brown achieved a rich texture by hammering into the metal with power and/or hand tools. Stephen Bondi used a range of rough and smooth textures on horizontal and vertical bars in his simulated woven fireplace screen. The handle is a shorter piece of a horizontal bar.

Michael Bondi. Oriental motif tree in repoussé copper with bronze wire cloth. Two leaves of the screen can be repositioned. *Photo, Colin McRae*

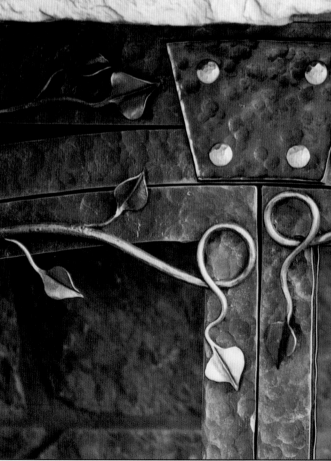

Bruce W. Brown. Leaves and curled elements repeat a wall paper design in a master bedroom and soften the textured frame of a pair of fire doors. *Photo, artist*

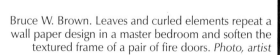

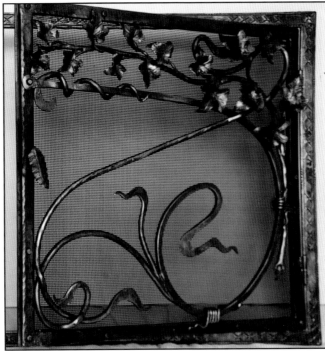

Stephen Bondi. ©Bondi Metals. Fire screen detail illustrating texture, and the ability to weave horizontal elements over and under vertical ones with hot iron. The handle and rivets are hand made. *Photo, artist*

Renato Muskovic. Art Nouveau design using an ivy motif was inspired by a photo in a book on Art Nouveau ironwork. Hot rolled steel forged. *Photo, artist*

217

Lars Stanley. A woven effect is achieved with all the horizontal bars behind the vertical bars bent so they remain in a flat plain. *Photo, Atelier Wong*

Lars Stanley also used horizontal and vertical bars but they were not woven; instead the horizontal bars were riveted behind the verticals but both sets of bars were bent to accommodate the others. Stanley's detail of a folding firescreen shows how horizontal and vertical bars were secured with angled bands. Hinges are hand forged.

Lars Stanley. Horizontal and vertical bars are joined with a collar on an angle in each row. The joinery becomes a repeat design element. Hinges are hand forged. *Photo, artist*

A detail of John Rais' "Dragonfly Screen" illustrates coloration, texture, and shaping. The bronze parts range from flat, to slightly curved, to heavily rounded, to create texture and sculptural dimension within a two-dimensional plane.

John Rais. Screen detail showing the smooth and shaped surfaces that contrast with the flat and textured areas. *Photo, artist*

James Viste used a non-traditional texture on a screen frame. The frame and interior bar textures emulate carving on a wooden African mask in the client's mask collection.

James Viste. The detail appears carved as one would carve or notch wood. The idea was to repeat a design detail in a wooden African mask. *Photo, artist*

David Tuthill. Screen with chain mail. The frame's dark color and chain mail pick up the colors in the stone fireplace. *Photo, Jay Dotson*

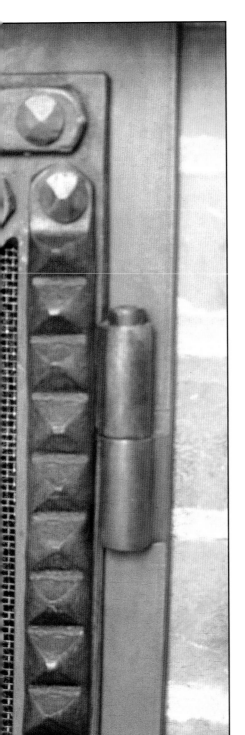

Frederic A. Crist and David W. Munn. Rich and varied detailing on the Leigh fire screen. *Photo, Frederic A. Crist*

221

Freestanding screens require supports. We have shown several throughout the book. Andrew Macdonald supports his screens with traditional scrolls in varying relationships to one another and to the support bars.

Screening, hinges, and handles provide the artist blacksmith with places to display ingenuity and mechanical expertise...or often just downright problem solving in a practical yet decorative fashion.

Christopher Thomson accomplished these feats brilliantly in an unusual hinge. Jefferson Mack pleated the frame and screening to create one dramatic detail in a screen.

Andrew Macdonald. Details of a fire screen support and riveted joinery. Mild steel. *Photo, artist*

Opposite page: Jefferson Mack. A "pleat" along the top of an otherwise unadorned screen. The resulting fold in the screen is the decorative detail that raises it out of the ordinary. *Courtesy, artist*

Christopher Thomson. An unusual post and hinge detail connects the three parts of this free standing fireplace screen. Wide open areas of mesh with courses of tightly woven areas give the unit added interest.
Photo, Herb Lotz

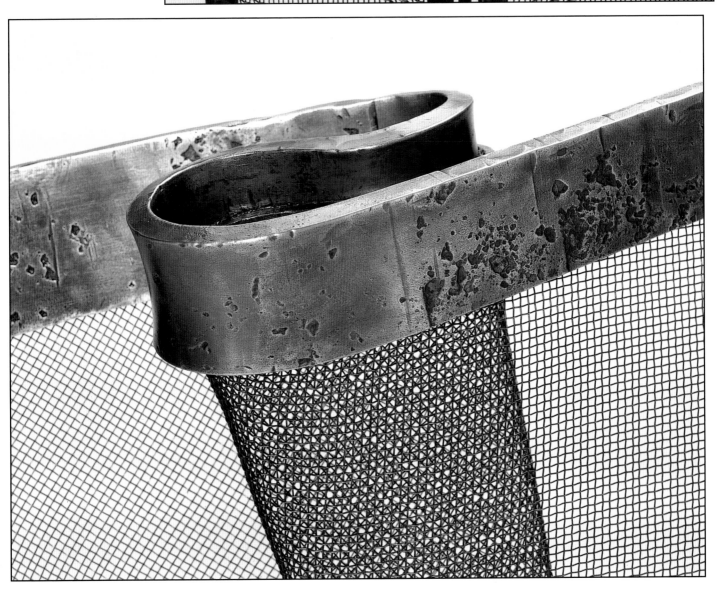

Hand made handles that enable the users to lift and move a free standing screen have to be easy to grab and, hopefully, not burn themselves if the fireplace has been burning. Most often they are placed at the top of the screen. Brian Gilbert's handle shown here is an example. Throughout the book, many solutions for handles on freestanding screens are shown. Permanently installed fire doors have handles for opening and closing the doors to tend the fire. They are usually in or near the center of a double door screen. Triple and double fold doors may have handles in the centers or along the edge of hinged folding doors.

Andrew Macdonald. Detail of a hand made hinge.
Courtesy, artist

Brian Gilbert. Handle detail for a freestanding fire screen forged from 1/2" round stock. The tapered steel, when evenly heated, forms graceful curves and spirals with a little guidance from the smith.
Photo, artist

Bruce W. Brown is a master at forging unusual handles and appears to find them an irresistible challenge. Twigs, twists, and graceful curves appear on his unique screens. Latches, too, are designed to fit the theme of the doors. Two examples of Brown's lift latches are so beautifully designed they look like pieces of fine jewelry.

Bruce W. Brown. Twisted handle with fishtail scrolls at top and bottom and hand made rivets on a hammer textured frame for a pair of fire doors. *Photo, artist*

Bruce W. Brown. Twig shaped handles with leaves at ends match trailing leaves and vine around the fireplace doors. *Photo, artist*

Bruce W. Brown. Another pair of twig handles. These are lighter weight than the branch and twigs on the front of the door. *Photo, artist*

Bruce W. Brown. A lift latch with fishtail scrolls on each end. The heavy rivets that affix the handle to the door are repeated in the rivets at the top and wherever such a joint is required. The lifter bar is split in thirds and each end is delicately scrolled. *Photo, artist*

Bruce W. Brown. A bronze lift latch with a fishtail scroll on both parts, and a hammered texture. The bronze color is warm and inviting against the dark background, and when a fire is lit. *Photo, artist*

John Phillips. A protruding textured handle ends in an easy to grab C-scroll that doubles as the latch and a handle. *Photo, artist*

James Viste. An angular effect in the details around the door frame is repeated on the handles of an enclosure inspired by a design on an African mask. *Photo, artist*

Fireplace Tool Set Details

It would be difficult to remain unaware or passive of fireplace tool designs after seeing the variety shown in Chapter 4. But studying design elements close-up will give you a greater appreciation of the artistry and workmanship involved. Focusing on details of handles, shafts, shovel shapes, and stands is like looking at mini sculptural elements.

Frederic A. Crist and David W. Munn's pieces should be studied for their attention to detail and exquisite workmanship. In the examples illustrated, look for the C-scrolls in the part of the stand that holds the tools. This horizontal bracket is riveted to the shaft and its bulbous design repeats the curves in the tool heads in all three of their examples. The ball handled tools and matching screens were made for one house and designed to complement the motif used throughout the residence, including the lighting fixtures.

Frederic A. Crist and David W. Munn. The rounded heads and other details help provide the necessary weight and grip that make the tools easy to handle. *Photo, Frederic A Crist*

Frederic A. Crist. Detail of a brass handled fireplace tool set. *Photo, artist*

Frederic A. Crist and David W. Munn. Detail of handles for a Victorian fireplace tool set. *Photo, Frederic A Crist*

Andrew Macdonald. Detail of a wall plate and the hook for a wall hung fire tool set. *Photo, Jeffery Bruce*

Alice James. Tool handles are worked in a pinecone design. *Courtesy, artist*

Dan'l Moore. Detail of fireplace tool set and stand with squares and twists, and hooks shaped from square bars. Extra detailing is worked into each square. Handles and hook ends have a small C-scroll at each end. *Photo, artist*

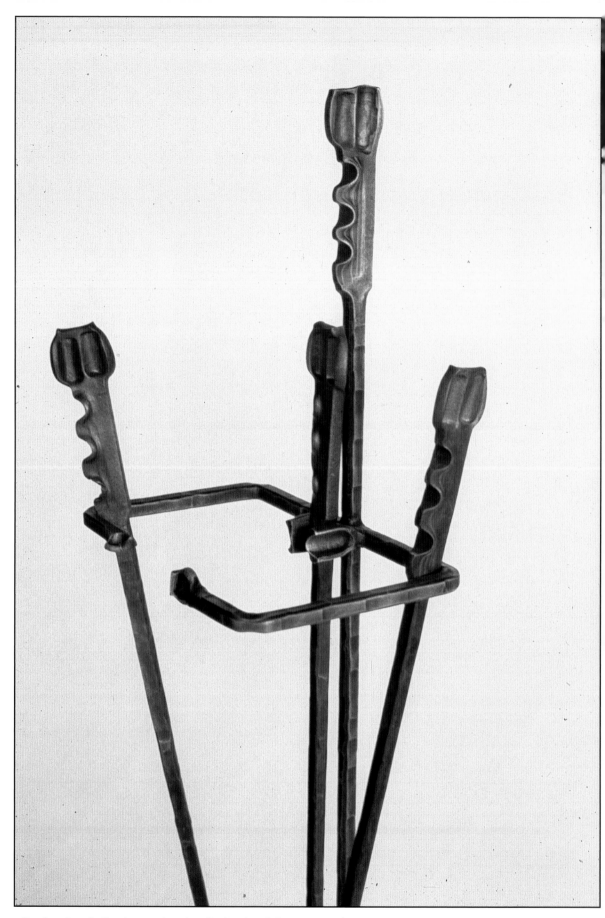

Stephen Bondi. Fireplace tool set handle detail with finger grips. *Photo, artist*

Stephen Bondi's tool handles have a fluidity and appearance that seems to defy the hardness of the metal. The tool holders appear as arms, and the tools are the people within being embraced. One set has finger grip indentations to make them easy to handle.

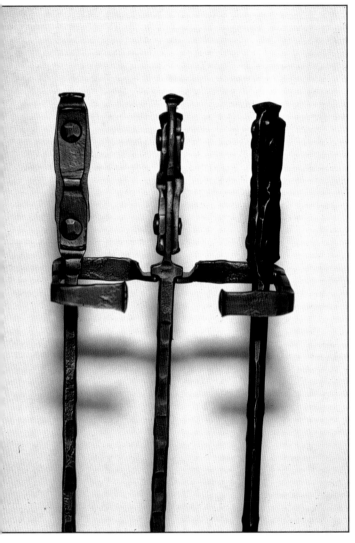

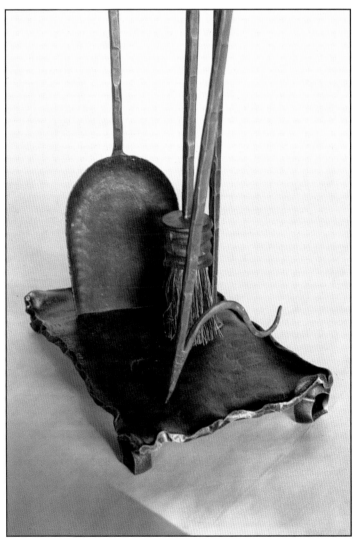

Stephen Bondi. Detail of a fire tool hanger rack and tool handles showing different sides of the handles. *Photo, artist*

Stephen Bondi. Fireplace tool set base with ruffled plate on circular feet. *Photo, artist*

John Boyd Smith. Base of a set of fireplace tools with heart shaped, notched shafts, and bronze rivets. *Photo, Rhonda Nell Fleming*

John Boyd Smith's tool base has soft ruffling and texture that looks like it was modeled in clay rather than hammered from metal. Observe how the shafts are notched for design and the bronze rivets are frankly enlarged for both design and function. Bondi and Smith use the ruffle detail on the base of their tool sets but they differ in appearance.

Andirons

The variety of treatments shown for andirons is stunning. Their details, too, reveal a craftsmanship and sculptural quality. Andirons that hold the wood or gas logs are subjected to high heat, so must be of heavier steel than tools and screens. Usually they are made to look as gutsy as the job for which they're fashioned. That can be seen easily on the andiron top by Keith A. Leavitt. The twist graduates from very heavy near the bottom to thinner near the top. The very top is pyramidal shaped, a feature of Craftsmen styling. Bart Turner and John Phillips' andiron details attest to the size of the steel bars that must be used, and the joinery techniques required.

Keith A. Leavitt. Detail of an andiron top with a graduated size twist and faceted ball top. *Photo, Steven Dunn*

Bart Turner. Detail of the joinery for "The Phoenix" andiron. *Photo, Richard Nichols*

Daniel Miller. Detail showing joinery and iron elements used to hold pieces together for the andiron, "Clytemnestra Eyes the King." *Photo, Weststar Photographic*

Opposite page: John Phillips. Detail showing the joinery in the wheat twist andirons. *Photo, artist*

Animal Images

Many artist blacksmith's are fascinated by the animals that can be fashioned by hammering and shaping hot metal. Making such forms takes time and patience as the hot metal cools quickly while it is being worked. Several heats may be required before the object emerges to the artist's satisfaction.

Andirons, fire tool handles, and screens show an exotic population of dragons, horses heads, rams heads, dogs heads, serpents, squirrels, rabbits, and other denizens of land and sea. Some are realistic; most are stylized, or as imaginative as the maker can conjure and create. They all have a whimsy about them that add to their appeal. Jerry A. Coe's dragon head is one of a pair on an andiron grate, see page 250. An artist forms these heads for any number of reasons. But Dan Dole and Joseph Anderson's friendly dragon, see page 251, came about because it was requested by a client whose children loved to play "Dungeons and Dragons."

Natalino, Allessandro, and Willy Zanini. Animal head with ring. There is one head on each end of the andiron grate. *Courtesy, artist*

Glenn F. Gilmore. Detail of one of two repoussé dog heads in sheet copper on a pair
of doors that also use the fleur-de-lis pattern, above, as a design motif. *Photo,
McNabb Studio*

John Rais. Preying mantis becomes the detail and the handle for a fire screen. The insect twists to open the latch. *Photo, Tim Thayer*

Bob Bergman. Mythical animal heads and Old Man Winter watch over the logs on the uprights of a log basket. *Photo, artist*

Roland C. Greefkes. Frog detail from the base of a free-standing screen that serves as a foot for the screen and appears that the frog is holding up the unit. *Photo, Aesthetica*

Robert E. Wiederrick. A flying duck with chiseled details is attached to the screening of a fire door and the duck appears to be "flying." *Photo, artist*

Jerry A. Coe. Close-up detail of forged bronze birds used on a fire screen. *Photo, artist*

Frederic A. Crist. Eagle head poker end forged. Collection, Vic & Ruth Ray. *Photo, artist*

Joseph Anderson. Squirrel tails bend and become the hanging device for the tools. *Photo, artist*

Frank Jackson. Impala head is one of a variety of animal heads used to adorn Jackson's fireplace tools and andirons. *Photo, artist*

Frank Jackson. Horse and cow heads. *Photo, artist*

Chris Axelsson. Serpent heads form wall mounted hooks on which the tools hang. *Photo, George Dukest*

Rod Pickett. Two matching rams' heads are on the upright ends of a pair of andirons. *Photo, artist*

Chris Axelsson. Horse's head on the end of a fire tool handle. *Photo, artist*

James Horrobin. Ram's head handle on the top of a poker. The rams' horns are made of a coil of iron. *Photo, artist*

Dan'l Moore. Devi's two-faced head has one face on the back and one on the front. *Photo, artist*

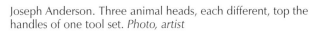
Joseph Anderson. Three animal heads, each different, top the handles of one tool set. *Photo, artist*

Frederic A. Crist. Three bishop's heads forged and carved for handles of a fire tool set. *Courtesy, artist*

Jerry A. Coe. Detail of a carved animal head from the andiron and grate, see page 151. One can almost imagine the smoke and fire spewing from the monster's nostrils. *Photo, Richard Sargent*

Dan Dole, with Joseph Anderson's assistance. Carved and forged dragon head for a fire tool set. The client's children loved to play "Dungeons and Dragons" and that was the inspiration. *Photo, Richard Sargent*

Bibliography

Andrews, Jack. *Samuel Yellin, Metalworker.* Ocean City, Maryland: Skipjack Press, 1992

Campbell, Marian. *Decorative Ironwork.* New York, New York: Harry N. Abrams., 1998

Innes, Miranda. *The Fireplace Book.* New York, New York: The Viking Studio, 2000

Johnson, Bruce L. *A History of the Grove Park Inn.* Asheville, North Carolina: The Grove Park Inn and Country Club, 1991

Kahr, Joan. *Edgar Brandt, Master of Art Deco Ironwork.* New York, 1969

Kauffman, Henry J. *Early American Ironware.* Rutland, Vermont: Charles E. Tuttle, 1966

Meilach, Dona Z. *Decorative & Sculptural Ironwork (Reprint Edition).* Atglen, Pennsylvania: Schiffer Publishing Ltd., 1999

Meilach, Dona Z. *Architectural Ironwork.* Atglen, Pennsylvania: Schiffer Publishing Ltd., 2001

Meilach, Dona Z. *The Contemporary Blacksmith.* Atglen, Pennsylvania: Schiffer Publishing Ltd., 2000

Plummer, Don; Brennan Cavanaugh, Jack Andrews. *Colonial Wrought Iron, the Sorber Collection.* Ocean City, Maryland: Skipjack Press, 1999

Sonn, Albert H. *Early American Wrought Iron (Reprint Edition),* New York, New York: Bonanza Books, 1979

Resources

Many of the artists whose work is shown in this book have Web sites and you can find them under their names or by doing a search. Several art galleries represent artist blacksmiths.

For artist blacksmiths in any area contact:

Artist Blacksmith Association of North America, ABANA

PO Box 206

Washington, MO 63090

314 390-2133

http://www.abana.org.

There are one or more ABANA groups in every state and there may be one near you.

In Europe, contact:

BABA, the British Artist Blacksmith Association

111 Main Street

Ratho, Newbridge, Midlothian. EH 28 8RS. Scotland

http://bab.org.uk

Hearth Products Association

1601 North Kent Street, Suite 1001

Arlington, Virginia 22209

703 522-0086

fax 703 522-0548

www.hearthassociation.org

You can also locate individuals by searching for their Web sites under any number of search words. If you know someone's name from a reference, use the name. Also, search under key words such as fireplace tools, blacksmithing, metalworking. Word of mouth is also a good reference. A few artist blacksmiths merchandise their skills by unique methods. Robert Wiederrick, for example, maintains a display case in a shopping mall and gets many clients from that resource. If you see someone's work you admire in this book, contact the author via the publisher in America or Europe. The publisher's address and e-mails are on the copyright page of this book.

Working Directly With An Artist

Different artists will have different procedures. Generally, after a contact is made, and the project is discussed, the artist will provide a rough sketch of the design. A deposit or retainer may be required to cover the time involved. Following a go-ahead from the client, a contract may be drawn up with a down payment expected. Final full scale drawings are rendered, the materials purchased (an additional fee may be contracted for at this point), and the work proceeds. Other items to be covered would be the finishes and installation. In some states, glass fire doors are a code requirement so metals, screening, and glass should be included.

Working With A Gallery

Several art galleries now represent artist blacksmith's work and more will do so in the future. When you find a gallery that handles ironwork, you may find exactly what you want or you may want to ask about commissioning an artist to create fireplace hardware to your vision and specifications. The following information about the relationship between a gallery and an artist will give you a good idea of how to proceed. It is offered by Lars Stanley who has worked closely with a gallery for several of his architectural ironwork commissions and the sale of fireplace accessories.

An individual who creates artistic and architectural metalwork as a full time career usually must diversify his/her marketing efforts to make a living. One way to do this is by selling pieces through galleries. This is especially suitable for elements related to the fireplace. Galleries offer an artist a much wider market than they can generate themselves, although there are some concessions that must be made in exchange.

Some galleries like to offer unique, one-of-a-kind pieces, others like to deal with smaller, less pricey, production items. Some galleries cater to the rich and famous, others to the everyday collector or holiday shopper. It is critical that the artist understand how his work will be presented, and how to work with a gallery satisfactorily.

The gallery, like the artist, is in business. The artist has costs involved for creating the work of art, as well as overhead and profit, which is reimbursed by the sale of the piece, plus his time. The gallery owner bears the expense of operating the gallery (which is often in a ritzy, high rent part of town), marketing the artwork it sells, overhead and profit, etc. This is reimbursed by the sale of the piece. Usually, the gallery will take the artist's price (sometimes called the wholesale price) and double it, which then becomes the sales price to the public. It is not uncommon for the gallery to more than double the artist's price if they think that the market will bear it. Sometimes, if a piece is very expensive, an artist may be able to negotiate a larger percentage of the final price.

All these points must be negotiated between the artist and the gallery owner. It is imperative to get an agreement in writing prior to shipping any items. Other considerations to settle include:

What type of marketing will the gallery commit to providing?

Will the gallery sponsor periodic exhibits or one-person exhibits for the artist?

If a buyer wants to hire the artist for further work, does the gallery get a commission? This is particularly important for metalsmiths who may be able to provide architectural ironwork through the gallery.

Who pays for crating and shipping? This should be covered by the sales price.

Does the gallery pay for the piece beforehand or is it taken on consignment?

If an order is taken does the artist need a deposit to start? (This is fitting as the artist has time and materials involved.)

How soon will the gallery pay the artist after a sale is made?

Clarify whether or not the gallery is to have exclusive representation and how far this right extends. Some galleries want exclusivity within a city or a region.

It should be clear that all copyright remains with the artist, especially if a line is developed and marketed through a gallery.

If the artist markets independently as well, clarify the relationship and agree on a mutual sales price so no ambiguities exist.

It is a good idea to visit the gallery and meet the owner in person to negotiate these points It is wise to record the agreement in writing and review it with an attorney prior to signing. Selling through a gallery may restrict an artist's one-on-one experience with clients but it should open up new markets.

Index